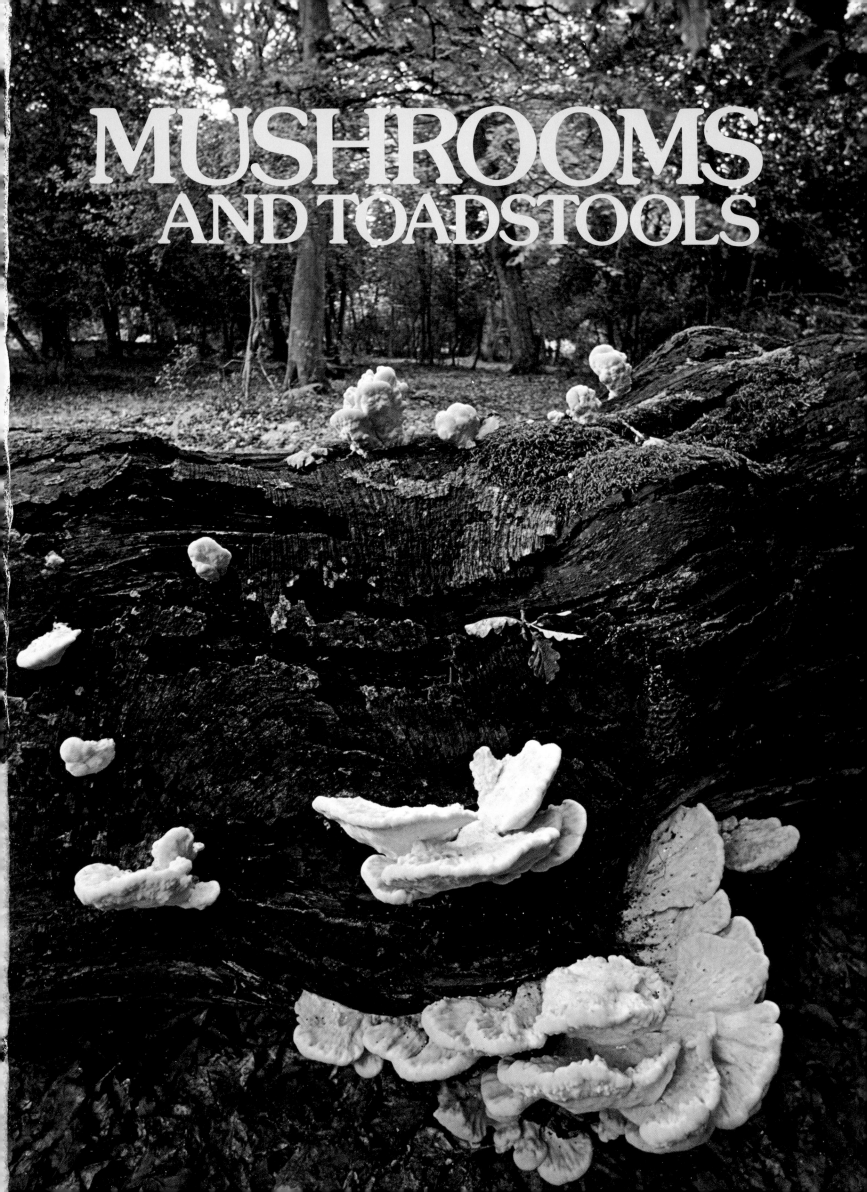

MUSHROOMS
AND TOADSTOOLS

MUSHROOMS
AND TOADSTOOLS

GEOFFREY KIBBY

CHARTWELL BOOKS INC.

CONTENTS

First published in the USA by
Chartwell Books, Inc.
a division of Book Sales, Inc.
110 Enterprise Avenue
Secaucus, New Jersey 07094

© 1977 Octopus Books Limited

ISBN 0-7064-0584-6

Produced by Mandarin Publishers Limited
22a Westlands Road
Quarry Bay, Hong Kong

Printed in Hong Kong

Endpapers: *Coprinus disseminatus*
Page 1: *Laetiporus (= Polyporus) sulphureus*
Pages 2–3: *Lactarius deliciosus*
Opposite: mushroom gills

WHAT ARE FUNGI?

The world of mushrooms and toadstools—the fungi—has always seemed a mysterious one to man; with their strange shapes and colours, their almost magical speed of growth and unique way of life, they have both attracted and puzzled him. Although fungi are one of the most successful forms of life on earth, they have for centuries been misunderstood and at times even feared.

Now, within the last century, man has come to realize the enormous influence that the fungi have on his life and upon the environment around him. He is giving them closer study than ever before and every aspect of their life, from their growth and genetics to their food value and chemistry, is receiving detailed examination. For the amateur, the collection and study of fungi can be one of the most fascinating and rewarding of hobbies. He in his turn can play a valuable and important part in accumulating knowledge of their habits and distribution, which are still in many cases poorly understood.

The study of fungi—known as mycology from the Ancient Greek word for a fungus, *mykes*—has all the advantages associated with other open-air natural history pursuits, plus others which are uniquely its own. Whether you wish to give them serious scientific study or just become acquainted with the many different species you can find in the countryside, you will find fungi an inexhaustible source of interest and excitement. For the artist they tempt with their beauty of shape and colour, while for the gourmet they provide new and subtle flavours. For the student of natural history they present the opportunity to investigate the unexplored, for there are always new species to be found and many gaps in our knowledge waiting to be filled.

As with any study involving plants and animals, there will always be the problem of names. Scientific names are written in Latin and based on Latin and Greek, and they frequently change as our ideas of the identity of a particular fungus are revised. This book therefore sometimes gives alternative Latin names for the same fungus, as well as any common names that are widely known. The Latin names may seem cumbersome, but they provide an international language for the naming of plants and animals which enables people all over the world to know exactly which fungus is being discussed, regardless of their own particular language.

The fungus kingdom is a very large one and estimates of the total number of different species are as high as 100,000! Fungi vary in size from the microscopic yeasts and moulds to bracket fungi a metre or more in width. The micro-fungi, although they do not attract the same attention as the macro-fungi—the mushrooms and toadstools—are nevertheless immensely important in our lives. Yeasts have been used by man for centuries to ferment his food or drink and today our beer and wine industries, as well as our dairy products, use enormous quantities of specially cultured yeasts. Moulds, as well as being a serious threat to stored goods by causing decay whenever the conditions are damp enough, have also provided, in the case of the *Penicillium* fungi, an invaluable aid in the fight against disease—the antibiotic, penicillin. Countless lives have benefited from, and even been saved by, this discovery.

Finally, anyone who enjoys the rich flavours of Gorgonzola

or Roquefort cheese has the fungi to thank; the distinctive 'veined' appearance and the unique flavour are the results of deliberate inoculation with moulds of the *Penicillium* type.

Some fungi do, of course, cause immense damage to our food crops—these are the rusts and mildews, and their relatives. Whether it is blight in potatoes, leafcurl in fruit trees or rusts on wheat, the results are the same—financial losses from crops ruined. One extremely harmful fungus is Ergot (*Claviceps purpurea*), which is a parasite on rye, some grasses and occasionally on wheat. Ergot also contains very powerful poisons which can affect both animals and man. In the past as many as 20,000 people died in a single outbreak of 'ergotism' after eating bread made from infected grain. Thankfully, with modern harvesting and cleaning techniques, plus the use of fungicides, ergotism is now very rare and instead the drugs within Ergot have been put to good use in the medical profession, especially in childbirth.

Fascinating and important as they are, the microscopic fungi take second place in the public eye. It is the larger fungi, the mushrooms and toadstools, with which most of us are familiar. There is, incidentally, no real difference between mushrooms and toadstools. The names are merely a matter of custom, with the word 'toadstool' being used for all those species which people *think* are not edible or are poisonous, and the word 'mushroom' restricted to that small group of fungi which are regularly eaten by man. The term 'larger fungi' is a very broad one and covers a great many types, both well known and obscure, but they are all large enough to be easily examined without the use of much more than a low-power hand lens. Before we go on to look at the different species, or types, it is important to realize the part that the larger fungi play in the environment and how they differ from the other plants around them.

In their methods of growth, feeding and reproduction, the fungi are different from all other members of the plant kingdom. Indeed, some mycologists think they should not be grouped with other plants at all but placed in a kingdom of their own. Thus one would have plants, animals *and* fungi rather than attempt to fit them in with other plants. The two essential differences between fungi and other plants are their complete lack of the green pigment chlorophyll, which is present in nearly all other plants, and their reproduction by spores rather than by seeds.

Chlorophyll enables green plants to make use of the energy provided by sunlight in order to convert into food the minerals and water which they absorb through their roots, plus the carbon dioxide they absorb through their leaves. Because fungi contain no chlorophyll they have to obtain their food directly from other organisms, either living or dead. Many are parasites of various plants, attacking their tissues and often eventually killing the host plant. Others form a close and beneficial association with trees, with both fungus and tree sharing various important nutrients and chemicals. This association is called mycorrhiza and is typical of a great many toadstools. Other fungi, known as saprophytes, obtain their food from dead and decaying organisms, thus playing an essential role in breaking down and digesting the vast amounts of organic litter which collect on the Earth's surface. You need only to think of the average woodland and of the amount of leaves, twigs and even whole trees which fall to the ground, to realize that unless something were removing this litter it would quickly reach enormous proportions.

The forest floor is therefore full of a mostly invisible mass of fungi which are slowly digesting and reducing the organic litter to its basic constituents. But this does not mean to say that fungi only grow in woods; they have, in fact, conquered every conceivable habitat and can be found in habitats ranging from deep coalmines to mountain peaks. This is one of the many fascinations of collecting fungi.

A fungus reproduces itself by spores rather than seeds, as a true plant does. The spores are extremely small—usually only a few thousandths of a millimetre in length—and normally simple single-celled structures, although their shapes and colours can vary enormously. They are often

extremely important in the identification of the more difficult species of fungi; such details as what sort of ornamentation they have on their surface, their length and colour all play a part in deciding just what fungus a mycologist is looking at.

For a spore to germinate, the conditions have to be exactly right, and the humidity, temperature and kind of soil all affect the growth of the spores. Of the millions of spores produced by the average toadstool—and it has been calculated that one toadstool can release up to several hundred million spores—only one on average survives to start a new fungus. Once it has fallen to the ground and germinated, the spore sends out thin tubes which rapidly branch and form a network, or colony, of threads. If you turn over some leaves on the forest floor on a damp autumn day, you may find these thin white or yellow threads running across the surface of the leaves and even binding them together. You may also find the same threads at the base of a toadstool which may lead you to the natural, but mistaken, assumption that they are the roots of the fungus. These threads are in fact the actual 'body' of the fungus, often stretching many metres under the soil and leaf litter. They are referred to collectively as the mycelium, and the individual threads are called the hyphae.

The toadstool itself begins as a thickening of tissue within the colony, or where two colonies of the same species overlap. This rapidly develops until all the important features of the mature toadstool are present, although it may still only look like a small button. When its growth is complete and the conditions are right, it will suddenly expand rapidly to form the fully matured toadstool. This can often take place in a matter of hours and explains how fungi appear so suddenly when it rains after a dry spell—the 'buttons' have stayed dormant until there was enough moisture for them to expand.

The toadstool's sole function is the production of spores and it is, therefore, only the fruiting-body of the fungus; it is the mycelium underground which is the actively growing and feeding part of the fungi. This is comparable to the fruit on a tree, with the toadstool as the fruit and the mycelium as the tree *and* roots combined. The mycelium may persist for years, while the fruit-body may only survive a matter of hours.

The larger fungi fall into several distinct groups, which although they can be quite different in appearance nevertheless have many points in common. Firstly they can be split into two major groups, or classes. Most of the toadstools belong to the group called Basidiomycetes. These are all those fungi in which the spores form on club-shaped cells called basidia, usually four spores to a basidium.

Among the simpler types of Basidiomycetes are the fairy clubs, which have fruit-bodies varying from single clubs to branched structures very like the corals found on the sea bed. Here the spores cover the whole outer surface of the fungus. A rather more complex type is the Chanterelle (*Cantharellus*) and its relatives. This is a very popular edible fungus which forms funnel- or top-shaped fruit-bodies with distinct wrinkles or ridges on the undersurface, on which the spores are formed.

It is the fungi with a distinct cap and stem, rather like an umbrella, which spring to most people's minds when the words 'mushroom' and 'toadstool' are mentioned. This cap-and-stem shape, with the spores produced on the underside of the cap, is common to many different types and has reached its highest development in what are usually called the gill fungi, or more properly the agarics. If you look at a typical agaric, for example the commercial edible mushroom, you will find that on the underside of the cap there are a number of closely packed, radial flaps of tissue. These are the gills, on which the spores are formed. The gills can be very important clues when trying to identify a fungus, as their shape and colour vary a great deal.

Yet another group of Basidiomycetes are the boletes. These fungi have the cap and stem typical of the agarics, but instead of gills they have a layer of thin, vertical tubes ending in pores, which form a sponge-like layer, and it is within these tubes that the spores are formed. Another variation is found in the hydnums, or hedgehog fungi, which have hundreds of dangling teeth, or spines which produce the spores. Many toadstools have dispensed with a stem and have taken to growing directly out of the side of trees and stumps, in particular the polypores, or bracket fungi. These very common, shelf-like fungi have pores very much like those of the boletes.

Finally there are the Gasteromycetes, which include the puffballs and their relatives. The rather strange name when translated means 'stomach-fungi' and refers to the fact that these fungi produce their spores *inside* their fruit-bodies. The spores are not released until they have matured, when the outer skin of the fungus splits or breaks open in various ways.

The second major group is the Ascomycetes, or cup fungi, whose spores (usually eight) are normally contained within long cells called asci. In both groups, the spore-producing

cells occur only on certain parts of the fungus and form a fertile layer called the hymenium. In the simplest cup fungi the fruit-body is more or less cup-shaped and the fertile layer forms a microscopic lining on the inner surface of the cup. In the more complex types of cup fungi, such as the Morels (*Morchella*), the cup is wrinkled and folded to form a sponge-like cap on top of a stem, and in these species the hymenium covers the *outside* of the cap. In the truffles, which are tuberous-looking Ascomycetes found underground and highly esteemed as a delicacy, the hymenium is folded and twisted *inside* the fungus, appearing as veins within the flesh.

Thus in each class of fungi, whether gill fungus, polypore, bolete or cup fungus, the essential aims are the same—to produce and release the spores as effectively as possible. What to us may seem just a curious shape or structure is for the fungus an essential part of its life and reproduction.

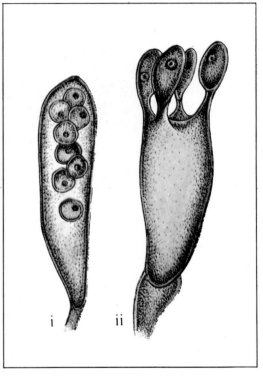

Above
Spore-producing cells
This diagram shows (i) a cross-section of the ascus showing the ascospores inside and (ii) the basidium and basidospores. The ascus, usually filled with eight spores, is found in the enormous group of fungi called the Ascomycetes, of which the cup fungi are typical members. In contrast, the Basiomycetes, which include the gill fungi, produce their spores *externally* on the tip of cells called basidia.

Previous page
It is amazing how much pressure an apparently soft toadstool can generate. Sights such as this, where a clump of inkcaps (*Coprinus*) are forcing their way through hard asphalt, are very common, and instances are known of whole paving stones being raised into the air! The slow, steady pressure of liquid rising in the tissues of the fruit-bodies provides the strength for such feats. Osmotic pressure, the technical term for this process, can generate many kilos of pressure across a few square centimetres of fungal tissue.

Above left
Marasmius species
The woodland floor is inhabited by enormous numbers of fungi, many of which are so small that they are often overlooked by collectors. The tiny ($\frac{1}{2}$–1cm) cap and hair-like stem of this delicate *Marasmius* make it difficult to realize that this is the same type of organism as the giant puffball shown on page 11. But, although they differ widely in their structure and habitat, both fulfil the basic function of digesting and breaking down organic material and eventually dispersing their spores.

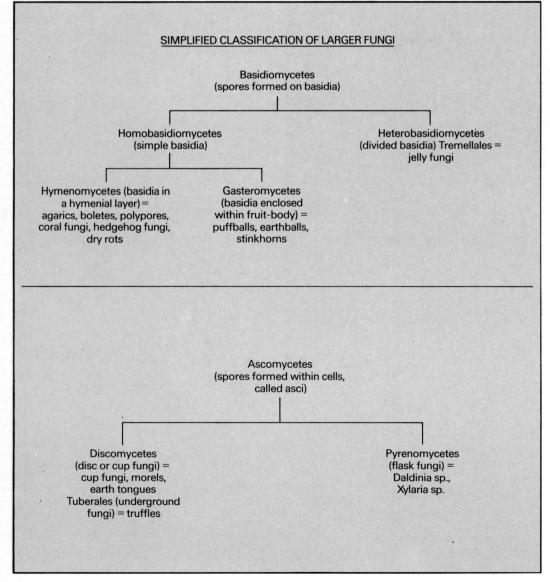

SIMPLIFIED CLASSIFICATION OF LARGER FUNGI

Basidiomycetes
(spores formed on basidia)

Homobasidiomycetes
(simple basidia)

Heterobasidiomycetes
(divided basidia) Tremellales =
jelly fungi

Hymenomycetes (basidia in
a hymenial layer) =
agarics, boletes, polypores,
coral fungi, hedgehog fungi,
dry rots

Gasteromycetes
(basidia enclosed
within fruit-body) =
puffballs, earthballs,
stinkhorns

Ascomycetes
(spores formed within cells,
called asci)

Discomycetes
(disc or cup fungi) =
cup fungi, morels,
earth tongues
Tuberales (underground
fungi) = truffles

Pyrenomycetes
(flask fungi) =
Daldinia sp.,
Xylaria sp.

Above
This diagram shows the underground
development of the mycelium, which is
the 'real' body of the fungus and often
covers an extensive area. The individual
threads of the mycelium, which you can
see in the photograph on page 13, are
called hyphae. The young toadstool
begins life as a small 'button' which lies
dormant until the conditions are right
for it to rapidly expand into a mature
fruit-body. Each fruit-body is capable
of releasing millions of spores, probably
only one of which will germinate to
found a new colony or mycelium.

Right
Spores
Although most fungi disperse their
spores gradually over a considerable
period of time, some discharge
thousands of spores at once. Examples
of this method of dispersal can be found
in the puffballs and earthstars, of which
one species, *Geastrum triplex*, is
shown here. This is one of the
Gasteromycetes, which contain
their spores within the fruit-body. A
central pore develops in the top of the
thick skin, or peridium, of the ball and
either the action of wind currents
passing across the opening or raindrops
striking the skin forces the spores to be
ejected. The dispersal of spores from
Geastrum triplex is one of the few
instances in which this action can be
observed with the naked eye, as it forms
a small cloud consisting of several
thousand spores.

Right

Lycogala epidendrum (Wolf's Milk Fungus)

The Myxomycetes, or slime moulds, are weird fungi which at one stage of their life cycle develop special cells able to travel along the surface of the ground, log or leaf on which they settle. When conditions are suitable, these cells change their structure and form small fruit-bodies containing spores. Because of their ability to move slime moulds were once thought to be primitive animals, rather than plants. Although most species are microscopic, some form quite large bodies; the species illustrated grows to 0.5−1.25cm ($\frac{1}{4}-\frac{1}{2}$in). The pale, pinkish liquid stage shown here matures to a silvery, globular skin containing the brownish spores.

Right

Serpula (=Merulius) lacrymans (Dry Rot)

This strange, pernicious fungus, believed to originate from coniferous timber in the Himalayas, is now associated almost entirely with man and his habitations and is rarely found in the wild in either Europe or America. For centuries buildings have been subject to the attack of dry rot, turning the timbers into soft, crumbling masses which easily give way under a careless step. The fungus appears as a thin spreading sheet, becoming orange or brown as the spores develop, with a narrow, white, sterile edge. Its tremendous growth rate is partly due to its ability to exude droplets of water which help to soften the surrounding timber and so facilitate its attack on new wood. It can also travel across or through structures other than wood, such as brick walls, by sending out special filaments, or hyphae, which conduct water to patches often many metres from the original area of infection.

Above

Mycelium

The thin, cottony threads which form the mycelium, the white fibrous matter from which fungi are produced, are shown clearly in this picture of a toadstool. This mass of thin cells is the actively growing and feeding 'body' of the fungus which spreads throughout the chosen food source, whether it be leaf-mould or decaying wood, expanding and digesting material until conditions are perfect for it to form a fruiting-body. The complex chemical and biological changes which take place within the mycelium can be compared in function to those which occur in the leaves and roots of a green plant, except that sunlight is not required for the production of food. The toadstool is only the fruiting body of the mycelium, just as the apple is of an apple tree.

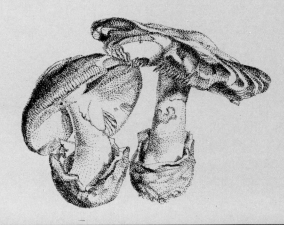

GILL FUNGI

The diversity of shape, colour and size found amongst the agarics, or gill fungi, can be bewildering to the beginner just starting to identify his finds. There are species which are so delicate and fragile that a careless breath almost blows them away and which, in any event, only last for one night and are gone with the first rays of the morning sun. Other species are large and robust, with caps which easily fill the average frying pan and sometimes even overlap at the edges! Some are exquisitely beautiful, with colours and shapes to match the brightest of flowers and often with hues unequalled by any plant—caps of flaming crimson or the deepest royal purple, delicate amethyst or lurid green; stems with coloured ring of 'tiger' stripes; fat stems and thin stems, pointed caps and round caps, and scales like the feathers of a bird.

Typical of the agarics is the genus *Amanita*, which contains such infamous toadstools as the Death Cap and the Fly Agaric, both notorious for their poisonous properties. If you look very closely at the very young, button stage of the Death Cap, you will see that it is completely covered with a white skin or membrane, rather like an eggshell. This is called the 'universal veil', and is typical of all the *Amanita* group, as well as many other toadstools. The veil protects the growing fungus until it is ready to expand and produce its spores. As the fruit-body expands and the cap lifts up, the veil is forced to stretch until a point is reached where it tears in two. The lower half, called the volva, is left as a cup or bag at the base of the stem. The upper half is left clinging to the cap and may split further into small flecks as the cap continues to expand. The volva is often an important guide to identification, as its size and form vary in different species. In the Death Cap it is distinctly cup or socket-like in form, while in the Fly Agaric it forms a series of ridges round the base of the stem.

Stretching between the stem and the edge of the cap, and covering the gills, several of the young amanitas have another membrane. As the cap expands, this membrane soon splits away and is left clinging to the top of the stem as a ring or collar. Once again, the presence or absence of this ring can be of help in determining identity. Instead of the thick universal veil, some toadstools also have a fine cobweb-like veil stretching between the cap edge and the stem. This is present in a great many toadstools but is particularly prominent in a genus called *Cortinarius*, examples of which are shown here. This very large group of toadstools takes its name from this cobwebby veil, called the cortina. Many species of fungi can also be distinguished by a gelatinous, often incredibly slippery coating on the cap and sometimes the stem.

All these characteristics, the volva, the ring, the cortina and the slippery, viscid coating, vary in the many different types of gilled toadstool and can be used to confirm their identities. The gills themselves are often very important in separating the different groups as they vary in the way they attach themselves to the stem. If you cut an agaric toadstool vertically down the centre, you can see more easily how the gills are attached. In the figure overleaf you can see that there are five principal types of connection and these are of real value as a particular toadstool will only usually have its gills attached in one way.

Despite the difficulties which may be experienced at first in confidently identifying some of the gilled toadstools, and indeed often because of these difficulties, they remain some of the most intriguing of the larger fungi. As a group, they exhibit a wide range of curious features, one of the most weird of which is luminosity. If you were to enter a tropical forest at night you might be surprised by a number of strange glowing lights on the trunks of rotten logs or even the forest floor. These would in daylight turn out to be one of the many luminous toadstools. In the tropics these weird fungi abound but they can also be found in temperate climates, for example one, the Jack O'Lantern, *Clitocybe illudens* (also known as *Pleurotus olearius*), found in America and the mainland of Europe.

The production of light by a toadstool has, not surprisingly, caused a great deal of amazement and comment in the past, and in particular, the fact that the wood on which the toadstool is growing often glows as well. Sir Walter Raleigh employed the simile, 'Say to the court it glowes and shines like rotten wood', and there is the now-famous quote of a soldier on duty in the jungles of New Guinea in the Second World War writing home, 'I am writing to you tonight by the light of five mushrooms.' The light varies from a garish green to blue or yellow, and white in a few species. Several groups display this phenomenon but it is especially common in species of *Pleurotus* and the clusters of delicate *Mycena* so common on logs are frequently luminous in the tropics. In temperature regions the most common luminous fungi is the Honey Fungus, *Armillaria mellea*. This parasite of trees attacks and kills great quantities of valuable timber every year, spreading voraciously by means of thick 'bootlaces' of densely interwoven hyphae. These can travel many metres underground to reach new sources of food, making this fungus very difficult to contain and destroy in plantations. It is the wood which glows but only as long as living, active mycelium is present in it, giving off a bright yellow-green or blue light.

A rather peculiar occurrence is the existence of two distinct strains of one species of fungus, one luminous and the other not. This occurs in the common agaric, *Panus stipticus*. In North America this is well known as a brightly shining toadstool, while in Europe it does not glow at all!

While the gill fungi excel in a number of curious features such as luminosity, in one particular field they outdo every other group of fungi and that is their smell. The variety and subtlety of the odours created by toadstools is astonishing; almost every type of odour, whether sweet, acrid, exotic or simply disgusting, is exhibited in one species or another. The genus *Lactarius* produces particularly distinctive and easily recognizable odours, such as coconut, curry powder, fish, oil, plus many others less easily placed. Other toadstools smell like apricots, honey, bananas, radishes, potatoes, soap, jasmine, aniseed and even cucumbers and roses! There is one fungus which although not an agaric is worthy of mention here as its smell is so strong and revolting that it has earned the name of Stinkhorn (see page 60). This is one of the few fungi you can locate from a great distance!

Closely associated with smell is taste. In many of our common toadstools there is a wide range of flavours which run from sweet, almost tasteless, to nutty, spicy, bitter, and finally those species which are hot and acrid. This is perhaps understating the case as some go beyond being merely hot and are positively strangling in their effects, leaving the careless mushroom gourmet unable to talk for several minutes! Even if you have established that your find is not a poisonous species, it is advisable to taste it with caution and thus avoid a rude and unpleasant shock.

Parasitic attacks by fungi upon other plants, usually trees, are very frequent, but some gilled species are specialized for attacking other fungi. *Volvariella surrecta*, a tiny pink-spored gill fungus is to be found, although very rarely, growing on the caps of old or decaying *Clitocybe nebularis,* another gill fungus. *Asterophora* (= *Nyctalis*) *parasitica* and *A.lyco-perdoides* have a similar association with old *Russula* species.

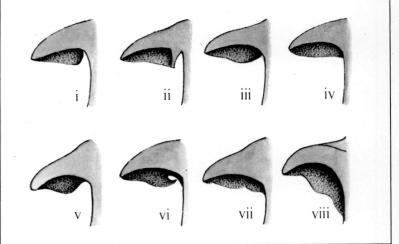

Above
The structure of the gills and the way in which they are attached to the cap is often a vital clue in identifying the many different species of gill fungi. The diagram shows the following main types of attachment: (i) free (ii) separated from the stem by a collar (iii) separated or near the stem (iv) adnate (attached) (v) sinuate (wavy-edged) (vi) forked or sinuate and margined (vii) decurrent, forming a tooth (viii) strongly decurrent. Cut the toadstool down the centre to see the gill attachment more clearly.

Left

The gills are the most important structure on the agarics, or gill fungi, and the whole fungus is shaped for their successful growth and use. They are situated on the undersurface of the cap, where they are protected from rain and falling debris from surrounding trees or plants. In many species the gills are additionally protected by a special veil of tissue until they are ready to function. They are arranged in the most economical way, with the spaces at the edge of the cap often filled with shorter gills a quarter or half the length of the ones in the centre. On the surface of each gill are thousands of cells called basidia which produce the spores. To ensure that the spores fall correctly, the gills are able to change the direction of their growth so that they are always perfectly at right angles to the ground.

Below

Armillaria mellea (Honey Fungus)

The Honey Fungus is the scourge of woodlands and particularly of cultivated plantations. As an active parasite and destroyer of living trees it causes enormous losses of timber throughout the world. It is found in dense clusters at the root of trees and occasionally, as in this picture, on the trunk itself. It will also fruit on fallen logs and old tree stumps. The Honey Fungus infects neighbouring trees by means of long, tough mycelial 'runners' called rhizomorphs which can travel many metres in search of new food sources. A very variable fungus, the finely scaled cap and woolly ring are distinctive features, as are the white spores. It occurs in a number of distinctive colour variations, which can confuse the beginner. When raw the Honey Fungus has a bitter taste which disappears after cooking.

Previous page

Lepiota cristata (Stinking Parasol)

As its name implies, this fungus has an unpleasant smell, rather like fresh rubber. A small fungus, only 2.5–5cm (1–2in) across, it is quite common in some years on grassy paths and even in gardens. It is easily recognized by the dark brown scales on the cap, ring on the stem, white spores and, of course, the smell. Some small species of *Lepiota* can be extremely poisonous, even deadly, so all of them should be avoided.

Left
Amanita citrina
This lovely species comes in two very
distinct varieties, a clear lemon yellow
and a pure white. The white form is
sometimes confused with other white
Amanita species, such as *A. virosa*, the
Destroying Angel, but the base of the
A. citrina stem does not have the tall
sheathing volva of *A. virosa*, instead
forming a very swollen bulb with a
narrow ridge around the top. Large
fragments of veil-tissue remain on the
cap and the irregular arrangement of
these gave rise to the old name for the
species – *A.mappa* (like a map). The
flesh of this very common species has a
strong smell of earthy potatoes and is
often helpful in identification. As with
all *Amanita* species, this fungus is not
to be eaten.

Far left
Amanita vaginata (Grisette)

This graceful and elegant species is very common in both Europe and America and is consequently one of the most well-known varieties of toadstool. Although it is edible and indeed eaten by many, it is not recommended because of the danger of confusing it with other poisonous *Amanita* species. It has the volva typical of many of the *Amanita* group, but it does not have a ring on the stem. The grey cap has a very strongly 'milled' or striated edge and usually has a small knob in the centre. The closely related Tawny Grisette, *Amanita fulva*, is more common in some regions. It can be distinguished from the Grisette by its orange-brown cap.

Above left
Amanita rubescens (The Blusher)

A candidate for the title of 'commonest toadstool', the Blusher is nevertheless the cause of much confusion amongst beginners, and even experts, as almost no other species comes in such a bewildering number of colours. The cap is usually pale brown, as shown, but it may also be white, pink, greyish, yellowish and all shades in between. The common factor of all these varieties is the reddish-brown stains which slowly develop, particularly at the base of the stem, when the fungus is damaged, as it often is by insect larvae. This feature has given rise to the common name of the Blusher and occurs even in the most untypical specimens. The species contains phallotoxin poisons when raw, but these disappear after cooking and it is widely eaten. However, I do *not* recommend it as it can sometimes be confused with the poisonous Panther Cap, *Amanita pantherina*.

Left
Amanita excelsa (spissa)

An extremely common species, this is a very variable fungus with a cap colour ranging from pearly-white to grey or brown. There is no volva at the base of the stem, merely a club-like swelling. The cap is covered with granular or powdery fragments of veil, and there is a thick ring on the stem which is strongly grooved on the upper surface. It can be distinguished from the related poisonous Panther Cap, *A.pantherina*, because the latter has a simple smooth ring and two or more distinct hoops or rolls of tissue at the base of the stem. Although not poisonous like the Death Cap, *A.excelsa* is not edible. It is found in all kinds of woodland throughout the autumn.

Tricholoma terreum

Tricholoma terreum is recognizable by its fibrous caps and stems, white spores and sinuate gills, i.e. gills with a small upward curve or notch near the stem before turning down once again (see the diagram on page 16). It is typical of a number of very similar species which have mouse-grey, fibrous caps and a white stem, and it is rather difficult to distinguish between them. Common in pine woods and occasionally in deciduous woodlands, they are often seen carpeting the ground or forming large fairy rings. Although edible, *T. terreum* can be confused with other poisonous species and should therefore be avoided.

Left
Laccaria amethystina
(Amethyst Mushroom)

Perhaps one of the world's loveliest fungi, a fresh, moist specimen of *Laccaria amethystina* is the most intense and glowing amethyst-violet in colour. The whole fungus is amethyst, including the gills, although the spores are white as in the other *Laccaria* species. When dry the cap is a pale lilac-grey and rather drab. As with the other species of *Laccaria*, although this fungus is not poisonous it is not considered worth eating.

Far left
Tricholomopsis rutilans

Commonly found on conifer stumps, this beautiful fungus is something of a puzzle as at different times scientists have placed it in various groups. Whatever its correct name, it is an easily recognized fungus, with a large, yellow cap overlayed with brown or vivid purple scales. The stem and gills are also yellowish, while the spores are white. An all-yellow or golden species, otherwise very similar, is *T.decora* which occurs in conifer woods at northerly latitudes.

Left
Laccaria laccata

An abundant and widespread species, found in damp leaf litter, on the banks of streams, grassy paths, bogs and indeed any woodland that is damper than average. The rusty-brown to pinkish cap varies a great deal in shade and depth of colour and can be confusing to the beginner, but the fibrous stem, scurfy cap when dry and pinkish gills are constant features. The spores are white, not pink as you might think from the gills. When moist, the cap is often marked radially with lines overlaying the position of the gills below, but when dry the cap is an even honey-brown with smooth edges and a scurfy surface. It is not a recommended edible species.

Right
Gomphidius glutinosus
This rather attractive fungus is
commonly found in pine or larch
woodlands. With its purple-brown or
grey cap, glutinous covering, deeply
decurrent gills and almost black spores,
it is easily recognized. The genus is
believed to be related to the boletes
and, although it lacks the pores of that
group, it is nevertheless similar in its
structure and development. It is
edible but not highly recommended for
eating.

Hygrophorus eburneus

Often found growing in large groups in mature, shady beech woods, this rather small white species has an extremely slippery cap and stem. Although it is edible, the flesh has a rather unpleasant odour and the slippery coating does not improve its texture. A similar species, *H. chrysaspis*, stains bright yellow and another, *H. chrysodon*, can be recognized by scurfy yellow spots on the edge of the cap, the top of the stem and the edges of the gills.

Clitocybe odora (Aniseed Fungus)

The sea-green cap and delicious scent of aniseed makes this one of the easiest mushrooms to identify correctly. It is one of the best examples of the many strange odours to be found among fungi and is very useful as a rather exotic flavouring in food dishes. It usually grows in quite large numbers in deciduous woodlands, particularly favouring the edges of paths or roadsides.

Clitocybe geotropa

The genus *Clitocybe* may usually be recognized by its strongly decurrent gills, white spores and funnel-shaped cap. *C.geotropa* is one of the largest species of the genus, with a cap some 13–20cm (5–8in) across and a height a little greater than the diameter of the cap. It occurs in woodland clearings and on the edges of woods, only occasionally in open grasslands. Closely related and sometimes confused with it is *Leucopaxillus* (= *Clitocybe*) *giganteus* which is larger, whiter, has a shorter stem and is often found in open pastures. Both may be eaten.

23

Below
Hypholoma sublateritium (Brick-red Cap)
This clustered, wood-attacking species often reaches quite large sizes compared to the more common Sulphur Tuft *Hypholoma fasciculare*, the caps often reaching 13–15cm (5–6in) in diameter. The beautiful, rich brick-red caps, with a paler, veil-covered edge, are a striking sight during the late autumn months when they appear. The spores are a clear lilac or violaceous-brown when seen in thick deposits which distinguish the species immediately from other wood fungi, such as *Pholiota* which has brown spores. It is highly rated by some as an edible species but disliked or ignored by others.

Far right
Mycena vitilis
As a group the *Mycena* species are very easy to recognize, but identification of particular species is often more difficult. The species shown here is typical of the graceful, delicate structure of these fungi, found in clusters on wood or leaf litter in woodlands. None of the *Mycena* species is valued as edible.

Right
Coprinus picaceus (Magpie Inkcap)
In common with other *Coprinus* species, the cap of the Magpie Inkcap dissolves rapidly into an inky liquid when the fungus is mature. This process, called autodigestion, is the Inkcaps' method of dispersing their spores. The spores at the edge of the cap are released immediately before the tissues dissolve, and this process continues right the way up the length of the gills until the cap has entirely liquefied and the spores dispersed. The advantage of this method of dispersal is that the spores are completely free of any obstruction, with not even the cap or gills to block their path as they fall! This rather uncommon species is found in beechwoods and can easily be recognized by the white patches of the universal veil that are left on the mature cap. It is not a recommended edible species.

**Hypholoma fasciculare
(Sulphur Tuft)**
The Sulphur Tuft Fungus is one of the
most prolific fungi to be found on old
stumps and logs and in a good year
often occurs in thousands. It is much
more clustered than the Brick-red
Hypholoma, and the rather pale,
greenish-yellow to orange-yellow caps
with distinctly greenish gills are easily
recognized. The spores are deep violet
brown and often coat the caps lying
below them in the cluster. The flesh is
very bitter and it is definitely not an
edible species. It can be found at almost
any time of the year—it is one of the
first fungi to appear after the summer
rains and often one of the last to vanish
with the winter frosts.

Stropharia aeruginosa

Green and blue are two colours which are rarely seen in fungi, and of these exotic species *Stropharia aeruginosa* must be one of the most attractive. The rather sticky cap is a clear turquoise-green, with traces of the white woolly veil clinging to the edge. The stem is white and also covered with woolly veil remnants. The green of the cap is soluble in water, so that you quite often find pale yellowish specimens where the rain has washed out the colouring. All *Stropharia* species have purple-brown spores and are usually considered as poisonous, although one very large species, *S.ferri*, is cultivated for food in parts of Europe. Nearly all of the species grow on soil, particularly if rich in organic material, such as rotten wood chips, and some are even found growing on pure sawdust.

Left

Coprinus disseminatus

One of the most charming displays of fungi is that made by *Coprinus disseminatus*, which often produces clusters of many hundreds or thousands of caps on old tree stumps, principally deciduous trees. It is easily recognized, partly by the enormous profusion in which it grows but also because each cap is only a centimetre or two (about an inch) high and deeply grooved almost to the centre. Unlike other *Coprinus* species, the caps do not dissolve into liquid, and because of this and other features it has also been called *Psathyrella* or *Pseudocoprinus disseminatus*, a very large name for such a small fungus!

Right

Paxillus involutus
(Common Roll-rim)

This is certainly one of the commonest species to be found throughout temperate countries. The soft, irregular-shaped brown cap, with decurrent gills bruising reddish-brown, is very easily recognized. The cap can be very glutinous during wet weather. Another very distinctive feature is the inrolled margin of the cap when the fungus is young, reflected in its name—*involutus*. This brown-spored species is sometimes eaten but is best treated with caution or avoided completely. It is found in all sorts of woodland and it is particularly common in damp birch copses and under pine trees.

Above
Galerina (=Pholiota) mutabilis
This is one of the few fungi clustered on wood which is edible, but as it can be confused with other inedible species a careful note should be made of its features. The orange-brown to date-brown caps are usually marked very clearly with a darker outer edge, becoming pale yellow towards the middle with occasionally a very dark brown centre, as in this illustration. The stems are marked by a distinct ring and below this the stem is clothed in small shaggy scales. The Honey Fungus, with which it is frequently confused, has scales on the cap and white spores, while this species is a brown-spored fungus. Some smaller, and rather more solitary, species can be dangerous so care should be taken if you are collecting them for food that *all* the fungi have consistent markings.

Right
**Pholiota squarrosa
(Scaly-capped Pholiota)**
The many species of *Pholiota* are nearly all to be found attacking wood, either living trees or fallen logs. They are often very specific as to where on the tree they fruit, and some species always occur high up, perhaps where branches have snapped off, while others, as shown here, prefer the base of the tree. This particular species will occasionally fruit higher up but is much more commonly found near the ground. The very scaly cap and stem are characteristic and it well deserves its common name of Scaly-capped Pholiota. Although very attractive with its yellow cap, its tough, rather distasteful flesh makes it almost inedible.

Agaricus augustus
Certainly one of the most magnificent
of the *Agaricus* species (the genus which
contains both the commercial and field
mushrooms), the large cap, covered
with tawny or golden scales, make this
fungus unmistakable. The stem is tall
and thick and is covered below the ring
with a woolly or scaly coating of white
veil-tissue. The ring is very large and
flaring and, in common with all other
Agaricus species, the gills soon turn
brown as the spores mature. A
delicious edible species, it is highly
valued by mushroom eaters everywhere.
It is found in both deciduous and
coniferous woodlands, but not in open
fields.

Right
Volvariella bombycina
A magnificent species, this fungi is
unfortunately rather uncommon but
when found it is usually growing on old
or dead elm trees. The most noticeable
feature is the large cup or volva at the
stem base, and the pale white or
yellowish cap is beautifully silky. The
gills rapidly darken to a deep pink as
the spores ripen and this distinguishes
it from other fungi with a volva, such as
species of *Amanita* which have white
spores and live on the ground. It is an
edible species, and the closely related
Paddy Straw Fungus, *Volvariella
volvacea*, is widely cultivated and eaten
in South-East Asia.

Left
Russula cyanoxantha
Another example of the colourful
Russula species, this one is easier to
identify than many others. The cap is
usually a mixture of lilac, purple and
green, while the gills are a creamy
white and rather 'elastic' or greasy to
touch. It is an edible species and worth
trying when you are sure of its identity.
The spore prints of *Russula* species
vary from white to egg-yellow and are
worth recording for identification.

Cortinarius alboviolaceus
The genus *Cortinarius* contains such a
vast number of species that only a
couple of the more common varieties
may be shown here. Indeed, they
deserve a book to themselves!
C.alboviolaceus is a rather stout species
of a lovely pale lilac or lavender hue,
with a bulbous stem and a slight knob
on the centre on the cap. The gills,
although pale violet or lilac at first, soon
turn rusty brown as the spores mature.
Found in deciduous woodlands,
principally beech, this species, although
edible, is not recommended for eating.

Left
Panaeolus semiovatus (separatus)
Only to be found growing on horse or
cow dung, this otherwise rather
attractive species can be amazingly
variable in size, sometimes only a
couple of centimetres in height and
sometimes almost 25cm (12in) or more.
This is a common feature of all dung-
growing species, where the size of the
fruit-body is directly related to the
amount of food available. Consequently
you should always be prepared to see
very different sizes of fruit-bodies
growing in these habitats. This species
has a grey or tan-coloured cap, slightly
sticky in wet weather and with a tiny
ring on the tall, thin stem.

Right
Cortinarius pseudosalor
Possibly one of the commonest
Cortinarius species, this very slippery
toadstool can be quite beautiful. The
stem is often deep violet below and
silvery-white further up, and the tawny
cap is curiously wrinkled. The cap has a
fine cobwebby veil at the edge when
young and as it develops the gills soon
become rusty-brown. It often occurs in
hundreds, especially in beech woods.
Several similar species occur under
pines and can be difficult to distinguish.
It is not edible.

BOLETES

Numbered among the boletes, the fleshy fungi with a stem and with tubes on the underside of the cap instead of gills, are some of our largest and most spectacular toadstools. It is by no means uncommon to come across a boletus with a cap 200mm (8in) across and a stem to match, the whole fungus weighing 1kg (2–3lb). These toadstools are found throughout the northern hemisphere and in the tropics, where truly enormous species are found. Giants such as *Boletus portentosus* can reach a diameter of nearly 600mm (2ft) and a total weight of over 3kg (7lb)!

It is not only in size and bulk that the boletes are impressive, their colours and textures are some of the most exotic to be found throughout the fungus kingdom and they also include some of the most delicious of edible fungi. In their habits they are particularly distinctive as they nearly all form a special relationship with trees called mycorrhiza, whereby each provides essential nutrients to the other. Some species of *Boletus* will grow alongside several kinds of tree but usually each bolete associates with only one, or sometimes two, species. Two very distinctive groups within the boletes are nearly always found growing in association with one particular tree species. Species of the genus *Leccinum* are usually connected with one tree species, either birch, aspen or one of the conifers. These fungi all have their stems covered with a fine woolly down or coarse roughenings, usually of a darker colour than the lighter background of the stem. Members of the second group of boletes, the genus *Suillus*, often have a glutinous transparent covering on the cap, and the stem is covered at the apex with tiny glands which exude drops of resin-like liquid, giving it a dotted appearance. *Suillus* is almost entirely confined to various conifers and forms the bulk of the boletes you will find in a pine or larch wood.

The rest of the boletes belong mostly to the genus *Boletus*, with a few scattered in rare groups. *Boletus* species are perhaps typified by the most famous edible fungus of all, *Boletus edulis* (see page 80)—this is the Cep, Pennybun, Steinpilz or any other of a great many common names used all over the world for this most excellent of fungi. Its fat cap and stem, the stem with a network of raised 'veins', are typical of most of the *Boletus* species, although in some the network of veins may be replaced by fine dots or stippling.

The boletes are an unusual group among the fungi because they include so many delicious edible species. Even those species which are known to cause upset stomachs are eaten in some countries after careful preparation to remove the aggravating substances. A few species of *Boletus*, however, although they are not poisonous are so bitter and unpleasant that they would deter even the most hardened of tastes.

Boletus edulis is gathered by the thousand every year in Europe and, as well as being eaten as a vegetable, is dried and processed to be added to powdered 'mushroom' soups. Another bolete, this time one of the *Leccinum* species, is a favoured and important part of the diet of Scandinavian reindeer, which will travel great distances to find it. If you are collecting boletes, you often come across specimens with their caps chewed and eaten by various rodents and deer.

Although the majority of boletes grow in mycorrhiza with

trees, a few members of this family have branched out into different habitats. Some rather rare species grow on rotten logs and stumps and one species, *Boletus hemichrysus*, is even found on sawdust. Another quite common species has become a parasite; not only does it attack another plant, it actually parasitizes another fungus. Appropriately called *Boletus parasiticus*, it can be found growing on earthballs. It actually invades the tissue of the earthball with its own mycelium.

One of the most remarkable phenomena of the fungus world is flesh staining and this is particularly common in the boletes. Since the earliest days of fungus collecting it has been noticed that some toadstools rapidly change colour when they are damaged or when their flesh is cut and exposed to the air. For centuries this has been used as a warning guide to which species should be avoided as being poisonous, but in fact many species which change colour are quite delicious and perfectly safe. A common example of a flesh-staining species is *Boletus erythropus* (= *B.miniatoporus*). If you cut it in half, the pale yellow flesh turns almost instantaneously to a deep and vivid indigo blue. Other species turn pink, pale blue, purple, black or red. Some species change colour very rapidly but others may take several minutes, and some bruise all over their outer surface while others are only affected on their pore surface or within the flesh.

This strange, almost chameleon-like, change of colour is caused by the entry of oxygen into the damaged flesh cells, followed by a rapid chemical reaction which creates the colour. Usually two chemicals need to be present to cause the reaction and in some species, where there is little or none of one chemical, no reaction can occur.

For most toadstools the type of soil is often the deciding factor as to which species occurs where. One group of very colourful *Boletus* species found mostly in warmer regions and associated with chalky soil includes a very infamous bolete, the Devil's Toadstool (*Boletus satanus*). This fungus has the age-old reputation of being extremely poisonous, but it does not seem to be such a terrible fungus after all and is probably just very indigestible or mildly poisonous, particularly when it is undercooked. Several other species of *Boletus* occur in this group, most of which have varying amounts of red in their pores and stem and a network on the stem. It is a shame that some of these beautiful fungi are not very common.

Like most fungi, the spores of a bolete vary in colour according to species, and you can take a spore print by placing the fungus cap on some paper (see page 76). If you are successful, you will get a rather nice deposit in the form of thousands of spots where the spores have fallen from the pore mouths. *Boletus* spores are usually varying shades of brown or olive, but some more unusual colours do occur, for example yellow, pink, purple and black. The more unusual spore colours, however, usually occur in species which are separated into their own special groups. Most of these are quite rare but one with pink spores, a bolete called *Tylopilus felleus*, is fairly common. This bolete can, if carelessly collected, be mistaken for *Boletus edulis* and if it is intended for eating the collector will get rather a shock. Although not poisonous, the flesh is very bitter and you can easily spoil a dish of real *Boletus edulis*. If you look at the two species more closely, however, you will notice several differences: the pores of *Tylopilus felleus* are distinctly pinkish, the pink deepening with age, and there is usually a very strongly raised network all over the stem. The colour of this fungus is an ochre-brown, as opposed to the rich toasty-brown of *Boletus edulis*.

One would expect that our knowledge of such a large and attractive group as the boletes would be fairly complete, but in fact a great deal of work is still needed to distinguish some of the more doubtful species and new species are described every year. One of the problems is that some of the species are very similar in general appearance, and it is only when very close attention is paid to such characters as flesh colour changes, cap colour, spore colour, the texture of the cap

surface and flesh, as well as the habitat, that it becomes apparent that more than one species is involved. It is here that the amateur can play an important part by making careful notes of the characteristics of the fungus *in the field*. So often the fungus is examined hours after it was collected, by which time all the important characters have faded and the species all look much the same. Look at your collections carefully, compare your fungus with the descriptions and you may find you have discovered something quite different.

Previous page
Suillus grevillei (= elegans)
(Larch Bolete)
This species occurs only under larch,
and even a solitary tree will often
have its accompanying boletes around
it. Quite unmistakable, this beautiful
fungus is golden orange or yellow, with
a white ring on the stem and yellow
pores. In one quite common variety of
this species, the cap is a deep, tawny
brown or almost chestnut. A much
more delicate, paler yellow species is
the rarer *Suillus flavidus*, found on
marshy ground below pines in the more
northern parts of Europe and North
America. Both species are edible and
the Larch Bolete is quite a popular
food.

Above left
Boletus parasiticus
This fungus is the most easily
recognized of any bolete because of its
unique habitat, actually growing on
another fungus—the Common
Earthball, *Scleroderma citrinum*. A
rather small species as boletes go, it
only reaches a few centimetres across at
the most but nevertheless is very
attractive. It has a rich cinnamon or
yellowish cap, with pores which turn
rusty brown or reddish in parts. The
mycelium invades the tissues of the
earthball and sometimes kills it.

Above
Boletus erythropus
A rather strange, lurid bolete, this
fungus is readily identified by its brown
cap and blood-red pores. The stem is
also red, and if examined with a lens
can be seen to be covered in red dots.
This distinguishes it from the related
B.luridus which has a red network on
the stem instead of dots. The flesh of
this bolete turns an intense blue when
exposed to the air, giving the whole
fungus a rather exotic appearance.
Most blue-staining boletes are held to
be rather suspicious as far as edible
qualities are concerned, and it is safer
to avoid them.

Above

Leccinum (= Boletus) scabrum

One of the boletes with a woolly stem, this very variable fungus is a rather dull tan or brown in colour with very soft flesh. It grows in damp spots under birch, and is widely eaten, although because of its texture it is perhaps at its best in soups and stews. It has recently been shown to consist of several closely related species and is a good example of how detailed notes on your collections can help to clarify puzzling species.

Top right

Boletus chrysenteron (Red-cracked Bolete)

This is a very easily recognized species, with a brownish cap soon cracking to reveal reddish flesh beneath. The pores are yellowish and the stem is coloured red or purple, either in part or entirely. Certainly one of the commonest of the boletes, it is rather variable and there are some quite similar, closely related species. However the red cracks are constant and are therefore the most useful feature to look for. As the weather becomes colder, the caps of this species take on a beautiful, reddish-purple hue and virtually cease to crack. This 'cold weather' form can easily be mistaken for other species. It is edible, but not highly recommended, particularly as it is usually infested with insect larvae.

Right

Leccinum (= Boletus) versipelle (Orange Cap Bolete)

One of the most common and loveliest of this group, the Orange Cap Bolete is found exclusively under birch trees, although similar species are found under oak and aspen. The cap often reaches 15–20cm (6–8in) in diameter and has a rich, tawny orange colour when fresh and a slightly woolly texture. The pores are greyish-fawn, and the tall stem is covered in very dark, woolly floccules. It is this latter feature which separates the genus *Leccinum* from the other boletes. It is a widely collected edible species, particularly in Europe. Do not be put off by the fact that the flesh changes colour when cut or cooked to violet-grey and then black—it is still very tasty!

Above
Boletus luridus
A very attractive species with a pale pinkish-brown cap and bright orange pores, *Boletus luridus* is particularly noted for the strongly raised red network covering the yellowish stem. Like some other *Boletus* species, the flesh stains deep blue immediately it is exposed to the air and this has contributed to its notoriety as a poisonous species. In fact it appears not to be so very poisonous after all, but it is believed to contain the same chemicals as are present in the poisonous inkcap *Coprinus atramentarius*, which cause illness when mixed with alcohol. It is sometimes confused with the closely related *B. satanus* but the latter species has a white or greyish cap and very stout stem, while the pores are usually a darker red. Both species show a preference for woodlands situated on chalky soil.

Right
Boletus versicolor (Red-capped Bolete)
A quite beautiful species, the delicate rose-red to purplish cap colours of *Boletus versicolor* are very distinctive. The stem is similarly coloured, while the pores are yellow, bruising blue. This fungus is invariably found on damp grassy paths near oaks and is often extremely common in warmer districts. The twin specimen shown here is an example of a very common growth distortion, found in many toadstools where two fruit-bodies have not separated.

POLYPORES

Almost everyone knows the flat, semi-circular 'plates' or 'brackets' which grow on treetrunks or from tree stumps and fallen logs. These fungi are the polypores, their name referring to the thousands of tubes which form the layer of pores on the underside of the cap. These pores are very similar in arrangement and function to those of the boletes and at one time the two groups were classified together, but it is now realized that there are very distinct and fundamental differences in the structure and growth of their fruit-bodies and that they are not in fact closely related. The boletes, with their soft, fleshy caps and the very short lifespan of the fruiting-body, are very close to the gill fungi; the polypores, on the other hand, have much tougher, woody flesh and the fruit-bodies often last for many years, growing new pore layers each year. Although the polypores do on rare occasions have a stem rather like that of a toadstool it is usually very eccentric, coming from the side of the cap rather than the centre. By far the majority of species have no stem at all and grow directly from the surface of a log or tree to form the distinctive shelf or bracket shape.

Many polypores not only grow on decaying wood but are actually active parasites of living trees, their spores entering the tree via a wound such as a broken branch or crack in the bark. This is why you should always seal off the cut surface if you remove the branch of a tree. If you keep a regular watch upon a freshly cut tree stump you will soon see signs of fungal growth; within a year or two all sorts of species will start fruiting, and among them will almost certainly be a polypore.

The effect upon a tree infected with a bracket fungus varies, depending on the species concerned: some fungi attack the heart of the tree and in this case the tree can go on living for a great length of time, often with a completely hollow trunk. This is a condition found very commonly in old oaks which are infected almost always with one of two common polypores and quite often with both. The largest and most spectacular of these two species is the Sulphur Polypore or Chicken-of-the-woods, *Laetiporus sulphureus*. This magnificent fungus produces enormous fruit-bodies and often has layers of brackets extending a considerable way up the trunk of the tree. As its name implies, it is bright yellow in colour and frequently orange on the upper surface, the whole fungus glowing with colour when fresh and forming one of the most attractive and easily recognized species. Its flesh is, incidentally, quite soft and edible. The colour remains even after cooking and provides an unusual addition to a meal; the flesh is best when young and has a quite distinctive and pleasant flavour.

The second of the polypores commonly found on oaks is one of the most fascinating and famous of the edible species, the Poor Man's Beefsteak or Ox-tongue, *Fistulina hepatica* (see page 48).

Unlike the oak, which can go on living for a considerable time even when it is hollow, other trees often suffer much more serious damage and quite often die as a direct result of fungal infection. The birch tree is a species which is very commonly attacked and killed by bracket fungi and in particular by one species, the Birch Polypore, *Piptoporus betulinus*, whose white kidney-shaped brackets are a very common sight. Each year it produces fresh fruit-bodies which begin as a small white swelling breaking through the bark of the tree. This rapidly expands to form the mature bracket which survives until it is killed off by winter frosts. *Piptoporus betulinus* is a particularly damaging species because its mycelium attacks the cells of the tree just below the bark, where growth and feeding are most active. The tree weakens and eventually dies and falls down. The fungus continues to digest the now decaying timber.

Some of the formations and textures produced by the polypores are almost unbelievable, and one which always gives rise to wonder is the Shining or Lacquered Ganoderma, *Ganoderma lucidum*. This remarkable species forms rounded brackets attached to the tree by a short stalk, the upper surface of a shining, polished red or chestnut, for all the world like a freshly lacquered piece of furniture. It is easily dried and keeps its gloss, making it a popular ornament of many collectors. Another much commoner species of *Ganoderma, G.applanatum,* is a parasite of trees. Its large rusty-brown caps, extremely hard and woody, grow over a number of years, adding fresh pore layers each year so that you can tell the age of the bracket by counting the layers. The spores of this species are a deep rusty brown and the trunk of the tree just below the fungus is often stained by the continuous rain of spores. For a long time mycologists were puzzled by a layer of spores on the *upper* surface of the cap, when there was no other bracket present to drop them there. It is now thought that a static charge develops on the cap surface and many of the spores are 'pulled' round onto the upper surface as soon as they exit from the pore mouths. This fungus is often called the Artist's Fungus as the white pore surface stains brown when bruised and it is possible to draw a picture by scratching the pores. Many quite beautiful and elaborate works have been completed upon large brackets, and when the fungus has dried the picture will last for many years.

The polypores certainly hold the record for size among the fungi: species such as *Polyporus giganteus* can reach widths of over a metre and can form enormous clumps of brackets at the base of trees. This particular species is easily recognized, not only by its large size but also by the black stains which develop if it is bruised. The flesh is edible with a reasonable flavour, but inclined to be rather tough except when young. A closely related species, *Grifola frondosus*, is much better eating and, when deep-fried in batter, the flesh tastes very much like meat. This very distinctive species also grows at the base of trees, particularly oaks, and forms large circular clumps of small grey caps all joined to a fleshy base, the whole fungus presenting an appearance rather like a large grey vegetable.

Not all polypores grow upon trees and not all the species are typically bracket-shaped. A few species may be found growing from the ground and these usually have rather cup-shaped, circular caps with a stem. A characteristic example of this type is *Coltrichia perennis* which occurs near burnt patches following forest fires. Like most of the toadstools which grow on the ground, it has a stem which lifts the cap into the air and thus allows the spores to drift away.

The shape of bracket fungi can vary enormously, depending on the conditions present at the time of growth. One can easily be misled by very young polypores as they frequently start life as a flattened 'crust' adhering to the bark of a log, only later developing the normal bracket shape. Some very curious shapes appear when a log with brackets growing on it has been rolled over several times: like most fungi, the polypores can change their position in relation to the pull of gravity, and once the log is moved the fruit-body will start to grow in a new direction to keep its pores pointing down to the earth. This power of accommodation is even more dramatic in the gilled toadstools—if you pick one and lay it on its side within an hour or so the cap and upper half of the stem will have twisted upwards to bring the gills back into a vertical position. Because of this adaptability you will often find logs covered in brackets all of which are pointing in different directions in response to the log having been continually shifted.

The texture of polypores varies considerably from thin and fleshy to hard and woody, but in between are all sorts of rather strange variations. One species, *Inonotus hispidus*, has a strange furry fruiting-body, a rich reddish chestnut colour, and its flesh often 'weeps' coloured droplets. Another is so soft and absorbent that its flesh can be squeezed out like a sponge and the copious supply of water used to wash your hands, very useful on a field trip!

Previous page
Laetiporus (=Polyporus) sulphureus (Sulphur Polypore, Chicken-of-the-Woods)
This bright yellow or pinkish-orange fungus is a serious pest to the oaks, and occasionally chestnut trees, on which it grows. It often forms very large, multiple-layered brackets, which sometimes stretch a metre or more up the trunk of a tree. At other times it produces a single, rather irregular fruit-body. It is usually at its peak during the late summer or early autumn months and, in America particularly, it is highly regarded as an edible fungus. For eating it needs to be collected when very young, before the flesh develops its typical rather sour flavour.

Left
Piptoporus betulinus (Birch Polypore)
Without doubt the commonest and most pernicious attacker of birch trees, this fungus is to be seen in hundreds in any established birch wood. Almost every tree will eventually be attacked by and produce the fruit-bodies of this species. The soft-fleshed brackets are typically kidney-shaped and, when old, become brown or grey before eventually decaying and falling from the tree. The soft, absorbent flesh has been put to many uses, including blotting-paper, to staunch bleeding, to smoke out bees, as a fire-lighter and as a razor-strop. Today it is still in use, cut into fine strips on which to mount small or delicate insects in museums.

Above left
Polyporus squamosus (Dryad's Saddle)
One of the commonest of the larger species of polypore, this species really can look like a flat seat or saddle and is quite beautiful. The tan-coloured, almost circular cap is covered with widely spaced, flattened dark brown scales and is attached to the tree by a short blackish stem; the pores are creamy-white and quite large. This fungus has a very strong and distinctive smell and an equally strange flavour, but nevertheless it is sometimes eaten, sliced into very thin strips and fried. It is usually found on the stumps of deciduous trees, especially elm and sycamore.

Left
Coriolus (= Polystictus = Trametes) versicolor
Of the smaller species of fungi which frequently festoon fallen logs in hundreds of small, multi-layered brackets, this species is perhaps the most common and the easiest to recognize. The caps are variable in colour, as the name suggests, and may be grey, brown, purplish or greenish in colour, but usually with a narrow white border to the edge of each cap. The surface texture is rather silky and the colours are distributed in distinct zones around the cap. The pores are quite fine and white or cream, like the flesh. This fungus attacks all manner of fallen and decaying timber throughout the year.

Overleaf
Polyporus giganteus
Truly a giant species, this fungus may be found growing in large overlapping groups of brackets often a metre or more across. It is always found at the base of trees, often beeches or oaks. The caps are pale ochre-brown with a rather grainy texture and the pores are white, bruising blackish in about 10 minutes. The flesh is quite tough but edible if the brackets are picked when they are very young. It has a rather strong, acidic odour.

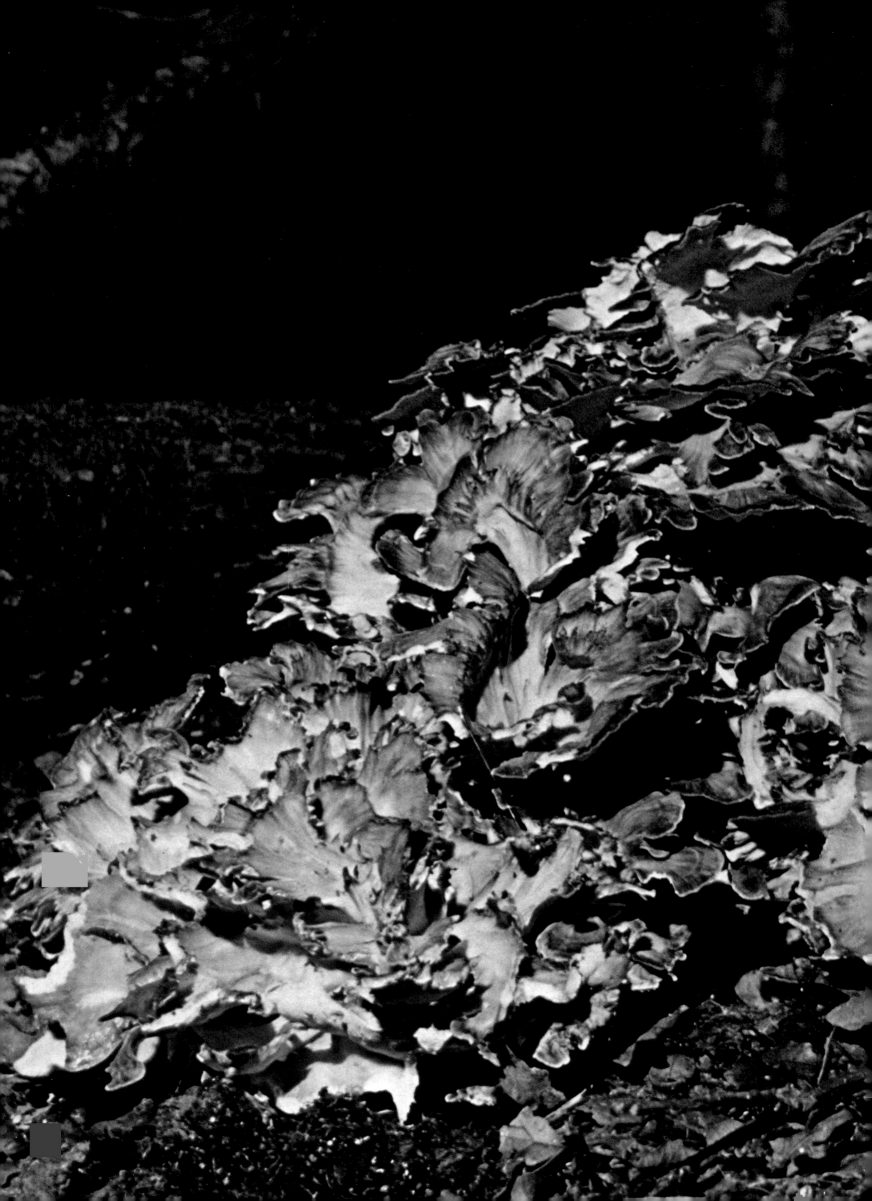

Fistulina hepatica (Beefsteak Fungus)

This curious species looks exactly like a large fleshy tongue or steak, and with its texture, colour and habit of 'bleeding' when cut it is not surprising that man should have made use of it as an edible species. In fact, opinion varies greatly over the supposed culinary qualities of this species, with some 'mycophagists', or mushroom gourmets, placing it very high in the ranks of edible species while others consider it tough and acid-tasting. There is no doubt that, like all fungi, it is best when young and requires slow cooking to render the flesh as tender as possible, and it certainly tastes unlike any other species. Whatever its merit as a food, this fungus serves man in another way, through its effect upon the wood of the oak trees it parasitizes. As the oak becomes infected with the mycelium of the Beefsteak the wood gradually softens and turns a rich reddish brown, and this red oak is highly valued in the furniture trade for its colour and ease of working.

Far left, bottom
Ganoderma lucidum (Lacquered Polypore)

This species is remarkable for the highly polished, lacquered appearance of the upper surface of the bracket. Often in beautiful shades of red, chestnut or purple, it is one of the most attractive of all the polypores. The bracket usually has a distinct stem growing from one side of the kidney-shaped cap and is to be found growing on various types of timber, including oak, chestnut and apple. It usually produces the fruit-body very low down, almost at ground level.

Left
Ganoderma applanatum

This iron-hard bracket fungus, with its thick, rusty-red fruit-bodies and white outer margin, is one of the commonest sights in any deciduous woodland. A very prominent destroyer of trees, it is a common event to find beeches still alive but with their trunks completely hollow and full of *Ganoderma* brackets. The surface of the wood below the bracket is usually stained rusty-brown from the billions of spores raining down on it for weeks upon end. The rather similar *Fomes fomentarius* is very common in Europe, also on beeches, but in Britain is almost entirely confined to birches in Scotland. It is distinguished from *Ganoderma* by being greyer in colour with white spores, while the bracket itself is usually more hoof-shaped.

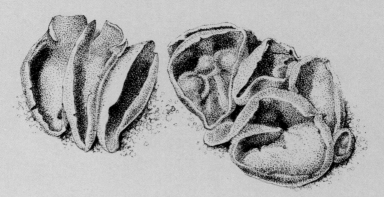

CUP FUNGI

The cup fungi, or Ascomycetes, form the second of the major groups or families of fungi. Unlike other fungi their spores usually develop within special cells, called asci, from which they are extelled when mature. These special cells are arranged in a layer or hymenium which lines either the inner or outer surface of the fruit-body, depending upon the species concerned. The majority of Ascomycetes are cup-shaped and there are many thousands of species throughout the world. Many are microscopic and often important causes of disease in plants. The species which concern us here are the larger cup fungi, plus the edible morels and false morels; the famous truffle, described on page 79, is also an Ascomycete.

The larger cup fungi mostly belong to the genus *Peziza* or to one of the closely related groups. They range in size from about 12mm ($\frac{1}{2}$in) to 30cm (1ft) or more in diameter, and they vary in shape from a simple flat disc to a complicated mass of chambers rather like a cabbage. They are not always easy to identify and for many of the smaller, less distinctive species a microscope or expert help is required. There are however some large common species which can readily be identified even by the complete beginner. Foremost amongst these must come the exquisite Orange Peel Fungus (*Aleuria aurantia*); if this seems rather an unlikely name you have only to ask any mycologist how many times he has bent down to collect this fungus only to find a real piece of orange peel, and occasionally vice versa! It is a clear, lovely orange and with its large, irregularly shaped cups does look remarkably like its namesake.

Other common and quite easy to identify species are *Peziza repanda* with large tan-coloured cups and *P.badia* with deep, rich brown cups. On old compost heaps you frequently see *P.vesiculosa* which has very irregular straw-coloured cups, often with a toothed or notched margin and swollen blisters within.

Cup fungi usually grow on rich soil or damp, rotten logs but some have rather more specialized tastes, inhabiting burnt areas such as old bonfire sites or forest fires. One of the most common species on such sites is the spectacular and beautiful *Pyronema omphalodes*. One's first impressions of this species is of a sheet of orange-pink mould stretching over the burnt soil, but a closer look reveals tiny perfect cups of the typical Ascomycete. Among the larger cup fungi such prizes as the lovely *Peziza violacea*, with its deep violet-brown cups, also like burnt ground.

Although only the larger Ascomycetes have ever been valued as food, one of the very small species was for a great many years of tremendous value to an industry. *Chlorosplenium aeruginascens*, the Green Cup Fungus, with its vivid blue-green coloration, was highly valued for its effects upon the wood on which it grew. Wood, often oak, infected with *Chlorosplenium* develops a green staining and the 'green oak' was used in the furniture trade to produce the famous Tunbridgeware, typified by highly decorative inlays of coloured woods, especially green.

The strangest of the *Peziza* species is *P.proteana*, *proteana* being Latin for 'many-shaped'. This species usually occurs as a large pale grey-violet cup, but very rarely a growth form appears where the cup erupts into a mass of interconnecting chambers and cups, the whole structure reaching the size of a football or larger. If you slice this growth across the middle, the chambers will be beautifully displayed. As the flesh is crisp and good to eat it is a shame it does not appear more often!

Apart from the more or less circular shape of the typical cup fungus some variations occur where the cup becomes uneven or lop-sided. This is typical of the genus *Otidea*, the Rabbit's Ear Fungi. Several species are quite common, the loveliest of which is *O.onotica* which is 75–100mm (3–4in) high and clear yellowish apricot in colour.

In late autumn a very strange fungus, looking rather like a large black button, appears on the surface of fallen trees and logs. If you touch the 'button' the fungus appears even stranger for the flesh has exactly the same consistency as a thick piece of rubber. This unmistakable Ascomycete is *Bulgaria inquinans* and you often see logs completely covered with masses of these rubbery buttons, each one surrounded by a black stain of spores.

On the soil and leaf-litter of the forest floor you may come across what at first sight looks like a dark green or blackish club or coral fungus (see the next chapter). These rather flattened, club-shaped bodies with a distinct stem are the Earth Tongues. They are usually species of the genus *Geoglossum* or *Trichoglossum* and it is only the club or tongue-shaped 'head' which produces the spores, the stem being sterile.

The morels are among the largest and most complex of the Ascomycetes and are widely sought after for food in Europe and America. Their structure resembles a cup raised on a stem and indeed some of the simpler species for example *Cyathipodia* (= *Helvella*) *macropus*, are exactly that and no more. This small greyish species has a simple stem with a shallow cup emerging from the top, lined with spore-producing cells or asci. More complex in structure are the species of *Helvella*, in which the stem is usually larger and chambered or fluted with ridges, and the cup twisted and folded to produce a rather saddle-shaped structure. Two species, the all-white *Helvella crispa* and the black or grey *H.lacunosa* are quite commonly found in the autumn and occasionally in the spring in woodlands and along hedgerows.

But it is in the true morels, the various species of *Morchella*, that the fruit-body reaches its most complex, with a fat, hollow stem and large spherical or conical cap, pitted and ridged with hollows to produce a sponge- or honeycomb-like effect. These delicious edible fungi only appear in spring, growing in woods, gardens and hedges and especially on soft sandy or chalky soil. The way the cap is shaped and coloured helps to distinguish between the species. *Morchella esculenta* is perhaps the best known and can reach between 12–26cm (5–10in) in height.

Differing in the way their caps are attached to the stem are the genera *Mitrophora* and *Verpa*, which are smaller than the *Morchella* species and also have a pointed cap much smaller in proportion to the stem. In *Verpa* species the cap is almost smooth, while *Mitrophora* species have a ridged and pitted cap very similar to the large morels. Although widely eaten, they should only be taken in small quantities at first until you are sure of your individual reaction to them as they have been known to cause upsets. Much more serious may be the effects of the False Morel, *Gyromitra esculenta*, with its convoluted, brain-like cap. This species has caused serious poisonings and should quite definitely be avoided even though some people can eat it with no apparent ill-effects.

The cup fungi are a very neglected group, particularly by the amateur mycologist. This, of course, is partly because most of the smaller species need microscopic study, but they are such beautiful and fascinating fungi that it is worth making an effort to get to know even the common species. If you do have access to a microscope, they are one of the most enjoyable groups to study in detail as their spore cells and the spores themselves make wonderful slides on which it is possible to see the spores being ejected from the individual cell or ascus. The spores are often highly ornamented with raised ridges and networks, and such features are often a decisive factor in determining the identity of a species.

The cup fungi are one of the few larger fungi which appear in the home and garden. Wherever, wood, plaster, bricks or matting becomes damp they are liable to fruit and some, particularly *Peziza domiciliana* and *Peziza cerea*, are apparently specialized for such habitats. Old houses, outhouses, woodpiles and so on often produce beautiful and quite spectacular displays of cup fungi.

Contained within the Ascomycetes is a large group of mixed fungi collectively known as the flask fungi, or Pyrenomycetes. These are distinguished by the spore-producing cells or asci being formed within deep pits in the fruit-body Flask fungi often differ radically from the usual cup fungi as they are frequently very hard and woody in texture, and either spherical or club-shaped in form. Typical of this group and extremely common is *Daldinia concentrica* (see page 72), popularly known as King Alfred's Cakes or Cramp Balls—the latter name in reference to their supposed ability to cure cramped muscles! These hard, black, round fungi grow on fallen logs and tree stumps throughout the year. Even more unusual is *Xylaria polymorpha*, Dead Man's Fingers, which forms quite large black clumps of 'fingers'. Also worthy of mention is the Candle Snuff Fungus, *Xylaria hypoxylon*, which looks like the wick of a candle with a black base and white upper half. This species sometimes branches to form an antler-like structure and then looks very attractive, with the white 'branches' showing up against the dark surface of a tree stump. It is sometimes the cause of root rot in apple trees and other plants.

Fungi can on occasion even attack animals and one group has specialized in parasitizing insect larvae. These are the species of *Cordyceps* which look rather like coloured drumsticks coming up from the soil. If you trace the stem far enough underground you will find it is attached to a larva. Other species of *Cordyceps* attack underground fungi.

As a group the Ascomycetes are as varied and diversified as any fungi and they are to be found in almost every habitat. For those with the patience and the facilities they offer a most rewarding subject for study.

Previous page
Sarcoscypha coccinea
Red is a very common colour among the cup fungi and it is best displayed in the small and charming Elf Cup, *Sarcoscypha coccinea*. As it often appears in winter, this beautiful species is frequently brought indoors on twigs and branches as a Christmas decoration. The woolly outer surface contrasts well with the bright scarlet of the inner cup, making it possibly the loveliest of all the smaller cup fungi.

Left
Mitrophora semi-libera
A rather rare but pretty species, this fungus resembles a thimble on a stalk. The name refers to the fact that the cap is only partially attached to the stem. The cap is brown with darker ridges radiating down from the centre and with cross ridges which produce a slight honeycomb effect. The stem is white and rather granular in texture, again with distinct ridges. Although apparently edible, it is rarely collected for food. This fungus only appears in the spring and is found in hedgerows, gardens and woods.

Below
Gyromitra esculenta (False Morel)
The False Morel is rather a dangerous fungus because, although it is often perfectly edible and delicious, it is not always safe to eat and is therefore best avoided. In the past, it has caused serious poisonings, and even death, due to the presence of the chemical monomethylhydrazine. The poison is destroyed when subjected to prolonged heat, but incorrect or insufficient cooking can leave a residue of poison which is sufficient to cause serious illness. The cap is distinguished by its strange, brain-like contortions. This spring-growing fungus can be found in a variety of woodlands.

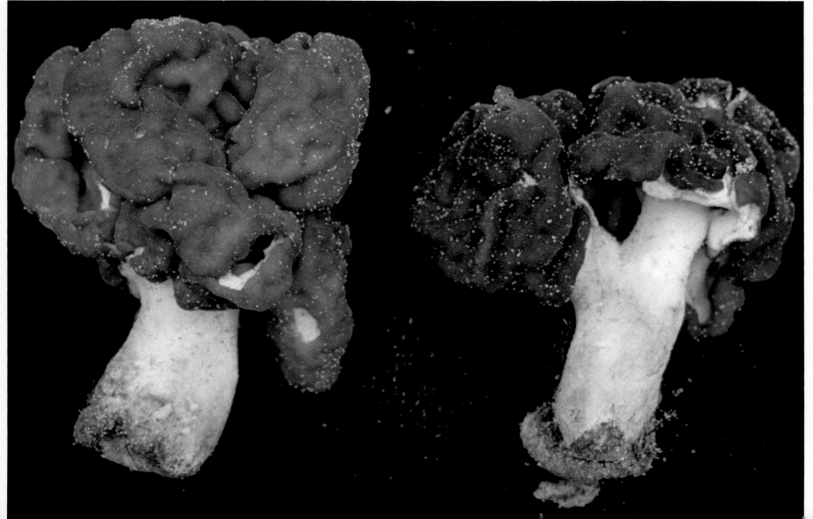

Left
Chlorosplenium aeruginosum
The mature cups of this species are not as well known as the green-stained wood for which they are responsible and which is used in the famous Tunbridge Ware inlaid furniture. This unusual fungi is found especially on old oak trees in the autumn, producing very small, 0.5cm (1/5in), cups of a vivid verdigris green.

Right
Helvella crispa
A delicate and beautiful species, in some years this fungus is quite abundant, appearing on almost every grassy path or river bank, while in other years, it is almost completely absent. It is quite small, only 8–10cm (3–4in) in height, but very easily recognized by the wavy, saddle-shaped cap and the fluted, deeply grooved stem. The entire fungus is usually pure white, although occasionally the cap may be fawn; the flesh is very soft and fragile, with the texture of thin wax. Usually an autumn fungus, it has also appeared in the spring and is often found with the related species *H.lacunosa*. This is very similar, but rather larger and the cap is more contorted. The biggest difference between them, however, is the colour, which in *H.lacunosa* is dark grey to black. It is regularly eaten by many people but should always be scalded first in boiling water as it belongs to a group which contains poisons destroyed by heat.

Left
Aleuria (= Peziza) aurantia (Orange Peel Fungus)
As delicate and beautiful as any flower, this vivid orange fungus fruits in profusion on damp path-sides, old bonfire sites and particularly near charred tree stumps. The flesh has the soft, crumbly texture of fine wax and the complete cup can reach 8–15cm (3–6in) in diameter. As with all cup fungi, if you disturb the fruit-bodies they will usually respond by discharging all their mature spores at one go. This rather dramatic display looks like a small cloud of steam rising from the cup and is accompanied by an audible puff or crackle.

FANTASTIC FUNGI

There are some species of fungi which do not belong to any of the groups discussed so far. They do not have the true gills or pores of the gill fungi, boletes or polypores, although some have the typical toadstool cap-and-stem shape. These fungi belong to such smaller groups as the hydnums (the hedgehog fungi), the club fungi, the stinkhorns, the puffballs, the chanterelles and the jelly fungi.

Of all these groups the chanterelles perhaps most closely resemble the true gill fungi, but a close examination of the underside of the rather top-shaped caps reveals thick wrinkles or folds of tissue rather than true gills. Instead of the very distinct cap of the gilled fungi, the chanterelle 'cap' is merely an expansion of the stem, usually very uneven or lobed. Many of the chanterelles seem to prefer damp mossy banks and shade, although of course there are exceptions.

Apart from the lovely egg-yellow Chanterelle (*Cantharellus cibarius*) so eagerly sought for sale in European markets, there are several grey or brown species and in North America a remarkable cinnibar red species, *Cantharellus cinnabarinus*, sadly absent in Europe. One species found in both continents and highly esteemed as an edible species is the Pig's Ear Fungus, *Cantharellus* (*Gomphus*) *clavatus*. This quite large species has a very uneven cap, tan coloured above but with the wrinkled undersurface a beautiful shade of violet or lilac, particularly when it is young. Less attractive and indeed often hard to spot because of its sombre hues is the Horn of Plenty, *Craterellus cornucopiodes*. This blackish-brown to grey species is widely gathered for food and has a spicy flavour which is useful as a flavouring.

All too frequently gathered in mistake for the real Chanterelle is the False Chanterelle, *Hygrophoropsis aurantiaca*. In fact this is a gilled fungus, very common in heathy woodlands under birches and pines and although it is harmless it is not very tasty.

The coral, or club, fungi really do look like clumps of deep-sea corals or small clubs, and like real corals many of them are beautifully coloured. The majority of species are only 50–75mm (2–3in) in height, they can grow as large as 15–18cm (6–7in) high and 30cm (12in) across. Some of the club fungi are edible and widely gathered; others are rather bitter and astringent and some cases of poisoning have been known, so you need to be sure of the species before experimenting. The simple club-shaped species vary from such 'giants' as *Clavaria pistillaris*, which forms a large brown club 15–20cm (6–8in) in height, to the lovely *Clavaria fusiformis* which is 50–75mm (2–3in) high and canary yellow in colour. *C.pistillaris* is frequent in beechwoods and *C.fusiformis* is found mainly on heathland soils under bracken and birch trees. The most magnificent fruit-bodies are produced by the coral- or cauliflower-shaped species, which at times it is hard to believe are fungi at all. *Ramaria botrytis* is a particularly handsome purple or pink species, with densely branched tips closely packed like the head of a cauliflower. Other species are bright yellow or yellow bruising green, among the latter the common *Ramaria abientina*. A very widespread and rather small species found along the banks of streams and on damp paths is the white *C.cristatus*, often found with a very similar but greyish species, *C.cinereus*.

Often grouped with the club and coral fungi is one very large and very tasty species which looks quite different. The Cauliflower Fungus, *Sparassis crispa*, forms enormous clumps on conifer stumps. It consists of very densely packed lobes or flattened branches, which form a large, almost spherical, creamy ochre mass very much like a cauliflower. The crisp, brittle flesh is good to eat, with a mild but pleasant flavour. A much rarer species, *S.laminosa*, with larger, more widely spaced lobes, occurs on deciduous trees, and is equally edible.

In all club and coral fungi the spore-producing layer (the hymenium) covers almost the entire outer surface of the branches or lobes. Because of this, the group is considered to be relatively primitive in contrast with the highly organized and complicated fruit-bodies typical of the gill fungi or polypores.

A very large and often spectacular group of fungi are commonly known as the hedgehog fungi. The fungi of this rather mixed group all produce their spores upon elongated spines or teeth. The many differing types of toothed fungi were once grouped under the one name of *Hydnum*, but it was soon realized that, despite this similarity, they were not all in fact closely related and many former *Hydnum* species have now been separated and renamed.

A very common *Hydnum* species found on the ground in woodlands is *Hydnum (=Dentinum) repandum*, which has the typical toadstool shape of cap and stem. This species is edible but its flesh is rather astringent unless it is boiled, and it is often better used as a spicy flavouring. Another ground-living species is the much larger Scaly Hydnum, *Sarcodon imbricatum*. This rather sombre species is common in coniferous woodlands and although the flesh is distinctly bitter it can be eaten after boiling.

Not all the toothed fungi grow from the soil and one in particular has chosen a very specialized habitat, pine cones. This is the Ear-pick Fungus, *Auriscalpium vulgare*, and it does indeed resemble the old ear-picks or ear-spoons. The tiny cap grows from one side of the stem, like a spoon with the bowl bent at right angles and with teeth underneath. Although quite a common fungus, it is frequently overlooked because of its diminutive size and rather dull dark brown colouring.

Many of the toothed fungi must be sought off the ground on trunks and logs and these species form some of the most beautiful fruit-bodies to be found in the entire fungus kingdom. Such species as *Hericium erinaceus*, *H.coralloides* and *H.caput-medusae* produce large, often huge, masses of varying shapes and with a varying number of branches of a pure, dazzling white. The teeth or spines are often extremely long, 10–15cm (4–6in), and the whole fungus looks quite startling in the shaded depths of a woodland. Some of these species are edible after boiling, but none of them are really common and sadly some are very rare. There are a great many more hedgehog fungi species, frequently with strange, almost overpowering scents such as aniseed or liquorice and some which are just unpleasant! Many are rarely seen and the correct names are often in doubt, but the more common species described above are to be found throughout the woodlands of temperate Europe and North America.

Passing to a completely different group, we come to the puffballs and earthballs. These very common and well-known fungi belong to the family called the Gasteromycetes (the stomach fungi) which produce their spores within the fruit-body, surrounded by a protective skin, the peridium. Most children must have either kicked or thrown them to see the dusty cloud of spores released as the ball splits open. Puffballs come in a number of different forms and can reach truly giant proportions, with the record find even being mistaken for a sheep at first sight! This specimen, about a metre in diameter, was *Langermannia (=Calvatia) gigantea*, which is frequently to be found growing at the edges of fields and in ditches or hedgerows. This species has long been a favourite of mushroom eaters for its large, meaty fruit-body is ample for several persons, the flesh being sliced rather like thin steaks. The majority of puffballs are edible—and delicious—when they are still in the immature stage before the spores ripen and become powdery, but the size of most species is less impressive, usually from 25–100mm (1–4in) across. The Latin names given to the puffballs, particularly the generic names, have changed several times in past years so that there are many species with two or even three names. The Giant Puffball, *Langermannia gigantea*, has been placed at various times in the genera *Lycoperdon*, *Calvatia* and *Lasiosphaera*, as well as being given different species names. But whatever it is called, it is an unmistakable fungus and certainly one of the most impressive you will find. A fruit-body of this size does of course produce a colossal number of spores—one estimate for a specimen 40 × 30 × 25cm (16 × 12 × 10in) was 7,000,000,000,000 spores! As this was by no means a very large specimen, totals in the region of 20–30,000,000,000,000 spores are not unreasonable. Luckily for us, the successful germination of a spore is relatively very rare or the earth would be soon buried beneath a vast mass of puffballs. On average only one spore per fungus will germinate successfully and so the numbers of fruit-bodies usually remains fairly stable with only occasional noticeable increases.

Many of the puffballs have distinctive warts or tiny spines on the outer surface of the skin (the peridium) and these spines are often very important in identifying the species. The presence of these spines is reflected in some of the puffball names, for example *Lycoperdon echinatum*, the word *echinatum* being the Latin for spiny.

Puffballs have various methods of releasing their spores—some species have a central opening on the top of the puffball where the spores are released, and in other species the spores are released by the gradual disintegration of the thick outer skin. It is partly by these different methods of spore release that the various genera are separated.

Puffballs are often confused with a very common group, the earthballs. Earthballs are rather similar in general appearance but they are usually tougher-skinned and warty or scaly, with the inner tissue often purplish and of an unevenly coloured, marbled appearance. The spores are released by the gradual breaking down of the peridium.

Perhaps the most remarkable and curious of the Gasteromycetes are the Phallales, or stinkhorns. These weird fungi reach their greatest diversity and beauty in the tropics but several species are represented in Europe and America. The commonest and best-known must be *the* Stinkhorn *Phallus impudicus*, a foul-smelling fungus with a strange, spongy stalk and slime-covered cap. It is frequent in summer and autumn in woodlands and sometimes in gardens, much to the distress of the owners! A related genus, *Dictyophora*, is distinguished by the beautiful lacelike veil of tissue hanging from the cap and one species, *D.duplicata*, is quite common in America although less so in Europe. The tropical species *D.indusiata* is a magnificent sight, with the veil hanging almost to the ground like the skirt of some exotic ballet dancer. Other Phallales assume even weirder shapes, some like starfish with blood-red arms and one species, *Clathrus cancellatus*, forming a perfect cage of interlocking arms, the inner surface covered in spore-bearing slime. This species is quite common in the warmer parts of Europe.

Very closely related to the puffballs are the earthstars which, as their name suggests, look very much like a five- or six-pointed star with a small puffball in the centre. As they are normally brown they are quite hard to detect, particularly before the 'star' has split open. The spores are released through an apical pore, like many of the puffballs. These fruit-bodies dry extremely well and make amusing ornaments, still able to puff out their spores even after many years on a shelf.

The methods used by fungi to disperse their spores are many and varied but none is more remarkable than that of the Bird's Nest Fungi, which belong to the three main genera, *Cyathus*, *Nidularia* and *Crucibulum*. These small fruit-bodies suit their name, looking very much like a

miniature nest with eggs inside. The 'eggs' are in fact spore masses, covered by a skin, which rest in the bottom of the 'nest', to which each egg is attached by a thin strand of tissue. The spores are freed by the action of a raindrop falling into the cup and splashing the spore mass out, often to quite a considerable distance. In some species part of the skin of the spore mass is sticky and so the 'eggs' adhere to plants or any passing animal, and may be carried a long way from their parent 'nest'.

Another type of Bird's Nest Fungus is the remarkable *Sphaerobolus*, a very small fungus with a star-shaped cup containing a single 'egg'. What makes this genus so special is the structure of the cup, which is composed of many separate layers joined together to form two membranes. Thus the cup has an outer and inner wall with a gap between. The inner wall, on which the spore mass sits, will suddenly flip outwards with tremendous speed and force propelling the spore mass up to 5m (17ft) horizontally and 3m (10ft) vertically! This natural fungus catapult can actually be heard when the 'shot' takes place. Sadly these strange fungi are not very common and they are so small and well camouflaged that they are hard to find. For those lucky enough to come across them they provide a unique and fascinating experience

Opposite page
Scleroderma citrinum (aurantium) (Common Earthball)
One of the earliest of the autumn fungi, this species continues to fruit right through the season until early winter. The orange-brown, scaly ball containing the strong-smelling purple-brown spore mass is a widespread and very common sight in any deciduous woodland, frequently growing in a circle round the trees and fruiting next to the exposed roots. The flesh is poisonous if consumed in quantities, but in spite of this it is eaten by some in small doses for its strong flavour and it has even been used as a substitute for truffles.

Left
Lycoperdon perlatum
This is one of the commonest species of a group which are known to almost everyone as puffballs because of the way the mature spores puff out in a cloud when the fungus is disturbed or struck in any way. This particular species has rather more of a stem than most other puffballs, but it is only the upper chamber which contains the spores. The stem is merely sterile tissue and serves the same function as the stem in gill fungi, that is to raise the fungus into the wind currents and so hopefully obtain better spore dispersal. Found in fields and indeed any grassy place, it is sometimes a nuisance on golf courses, being a wonderful mimic of a golfball!

Previous page
Ramaria species (Coral Fungus)
Many of the species in this genus are beautifully coloured, often in pink, purple or yellow. The many finely divided branches are usually connected by a stout stalk and the spores are produced on the outer surface of the branches. Some species are edible but others are definitely upsetting.

Mutinus caninus
A much smaller, and rather more
attractive, relative of the Common
Stinkhorn, this is often almost odourless
to man although it still succeeds in
attracting flies. The sharply pointed
stem is a bright orange, covered at first
by the green spore mass. At the base of
the stem are the remnants of the egg
from which it emerged. In warm years
it is quite common in woodlands and
gardens and does not appear to be so
dependent upon dead wood as its larger
relative.

Below left
Phallus impudicus (Common Stinkhorn)

Very common in late summer and throughout the autumn, this fungus first signals its presence by its foul odour, which often carries a great distance; this is one of the few fungi you hunt by smell! Nearly always connected to dead wood, it often fruits in rings around tree stumps and presents a rather weird sight, usually with large numbers of flies feeding on the slime-covered cap. It is interesting (if rather anti-social) to collect an 'egg' of this fungus and hatch it under a glass jar. The whole process only takes a few hours, usually during the night or early morning.

Below
Cordyceps militaris

Not all fungi are vegetarian in their diet and some species specialize in attacking insects or their larvae. If you trace the small, brightly coloured 'drumsticks' of this species down into the soil you will find the buried larvae on which it is preying. *Cordyceps militaris* is one of the Pyrenomycetes, or flask fungi, in which the spore-containing cells (the asci) are embedded right inside the fruit-body, with only the tips exposed. Other fungi attack flies or spiders, usually killing them.

Calocera viscosa (Staghorn Fungus)
A small but very attractive fungus, this
late autumn- and winter-growing
fungus is found on old stumps and logs
of coniferous trees. The yellow or
orange branches are soft and slightly
sticky when moist, but if they dry out
they turn dark orange brown and
become very hard, only to revive again
if remoistened.

Right
**Cantharellus cinereus
(Grey Chanterelle)**
A less famous relative of the true
Chanterelle, this is nevertheless an
edible and quite delicious species.
Rather smaller and more delicate than
the yellow species, it is coloured a pale
ash-grey. It occurs in the same damp,
mossy woodlands as the true
Chanterelle but is less common.

Far left, top
Anthurus aseroiformis
A strangely animal-like fungus, this beautiful species is a relative of the Cage Fungus, *Clathrus cancellatus*, and the other stinkhorns. Like them, it also pushes out from within an enclosing 'egg' and the inner surface of the vivid carmine-red arms is covered with spore-laden mucus. The distribution of this fungus, although widespread, is strangely sporadic. It is common in the Far East, Australia and New Zealand and also occurs in many parts of Europe, including Great Britain, although it must be considered a rare prize in these temperate regions. Similar species, for example *Pseudocolus schellenbergiae* and *Lysurus borealis*, are found in North America.

Left
Clathrus cancellatus (Cage Fungus)
This is a unique fungus, and quite unmistakable. The Phallales, or stinkhorns as they are commonly called, are most prominent in the tropics, but a few species occur in the temperate regions and this particular species is found in the warmer regions of Europe and America. The strange cage, or net, starts off life enclosed in an 'egg', as do all Phallales. When the conditions are right they will rapidly expand in a few hours to full size. The inside of the cage is smeared with a spore-bearing 'slime', which relies on its foul smell to attract flies. In their mature stage, stinkhorns are often distinguishable by the flies feeding on this slimy layer. The spores pass through the fly's body unharmed, to later germinate in a new locality.

Far left, bottom
Clavaria species
Clavaria come in a wide range of shapes and sizes, ranging from a single, simple club to a branched, complex cluster. They include some of the most fantastic fungi, often occurring in clear, bright shades of yellow, orange or pure white. They occupy a variety of habitats, from heathland to deep woodland. As with all club fungi, the spores are formed on the entire outer surface of the club.

Hericium (= Hydnum = Dryodon) coralloides

Although most fungi grow on the ground or at the base of trees, you should also look upwards on your fungi forays. You may find one of the hedgehog fungi, such as this beautiful and spectacular *Hericium* species. The dazzling pure-white and densely branched fruit-body bears thousands of pendant spines of teeth, on which the spores are produced. It is found mainly upon beech trees although it occasionally grows on oak, elm or ash. The whole fungus can reach diameters of up to 30cm (12in). The flesh is rather bitter but this disappears with boiling.

Top left

Sparassis crispa (Cauliflower Fungus)

A large and often quite beautiful fungus, this species is found only on pines, colonizing dead or weakened timber. The large, round fruit-bodies look very much like cauliflowers or sponges and are composed of hundreds of flattened and curled lobes packed together. They are, in fact, related to the club fungi although radically different in shape. The flesh is crisp and delicious, particularly when young, and it is not easily mistaken for anything else.

Left

Geastrum triplex (Common Earthstar)

If you come across what looks rather like a brown onion splitting into a star, you will almost certainly have found one of the earthstars. As you can see in the picture they have the typical puffball structure in the middle, containing the spores which will be expelled by the action of raindrops or wind currents. Earthstars are very frequent in old beech woodlands but they are very well camouflaged among the fallen leaves and can be difficult to spot.

MUSHROOM MYTHOLOGY

Since man first began to reason he has attempted to find explanations for the many strange events that occur in the world around him. Some of these explanations may seem to us, in the light of contemporary knowledge, to be almost as strange as the events they attempt to explain. It seems hard to believe that only a century or two ago scientific thought and myth were so closely entwined as to give rise to the many different, and to us amusing, stories that make up that strangest of fungal growths—the fairy ring. Often on a grass lawn or pastureland you can see a curious formation where darker circles of grass stand out from the rest, often with a circle of bare ground just inside the rich outer ring. Several rings can occur on a single lawn and often overlap each other, their size varying from 25–50cm (1–2ft) across to some more than 50m (55yd) in diameter. At the edge of these rings if the season is favourable you often find a number of toadstools.

Several different species of fungi form fairy rings but the commonest by far is that plague of golf courses, the Fairy Ring Champignon, *Marasmius oreades*. This tough, rather small, plain ochre-brown toadstool is found throughout the world wherever there are grasslands and causes more damage to lawns than almost any other toadstool.

In earlier centuries this uncanny formation was the cause of much wonder. What caused the ring of taller, darker grass? What was the meaning of the bare, worn circle just inside, with perhaps another richer circle within it? The bare ring looked suspiciously like the path of pattering feet and the rich grass could only be the result of spellmaking! One has only to look at some of the names given to these rings to see the explanation that appealed most to our forebears— fairy rings, fairy dances and fairy courts, hag tracks or the sorcerer's ring. At a time when elves and witches were 'real' entities, it was only natural to assume that they had performed their wild dances and revels in a circle under the light of the moon. Because of this belief in their magical origins, many superstitions have always been attached to fairy rings. Depending upon where you live, it can either be very good or very bad luck to enter a ring, and the dew off the grass circle makes a good love potion for young girls. To have a ring in the field next to your house can bring good fortune, but to let your animals eat the grass is asking for trouble!

The presence of the toadstools seems either to have been ignored or used as further evidence of magical or devilish influences, fungi being generally regarded with awe and suspicion. As the centuries progressed and more scientific and rational ideas took the place of superstition, such explanations simply wouldn't suffice, and so new, more sensible explanations were put forward by the naturalists of the day. The most popular and persistent of these was that the rings were the result of lightning. When the lightning hit the ground, the electrical energy was believed to radiate outwards, scorching the soil and thus leaving a bare circle. Other interpretations made use of all sorts of miscellaneous animals from snails to goats, the only point they had in common being that they had all been observed at some time going round in circles!

The real cause of the rings is of course the fungi but the circles are still fascinating structures, even if their creation is not quite as exciting as was once thought. The circular pattern originates when a fungal spore germinates and the mycelium begins to spread outward from this central point. If there are no obstructions, it will radiate outwards evenly to form a circle. Where the mycelium is thickest, the hyphal threads of which it is composed fill the minute air spaces in the soil and prevent free drainage of water. The roots of the grass suffer from waterlogging and lack of oxygen and so the grass begins to die, forming the bare ring. At the outer edge of the spreading mycelium, the soil is still clear and it has the added boost of various nutrient chemicals released by the fungus. The grass at this outer edge finds it has more food and so grows taller and richer than the rest. We now have the outer dark ring and the inner bare ring, but what about the other rich circle of grass that often appears within this? The answer is that the mycelium is only actively growing at the edge and the original central growth gradually dies away. This in turn reopens the air spaces in the soil, and the decaying fungal mycelium provides food for the grass that has survived or reseeded within the ring. With more food and oxygen, the grass is once more able to thrive and so a central circle of richer grass is formed.

It is strange that this idea should have taken so long to be accepted, particularly when it is known that one William Withering had stated as long ago as 1792 that fungi were responsible for the rings. The other, more fanciful, stories still held sway however and it was not until the mid-nineteenth century that the true facts were generally known and accepted by the majority of people. The true explanation does contain one amazing fact, however, which is worth remembering whenever we tend to mistakenly think of fungi as short-lived, ephemeral plants. The age of some of the largest rings, those 50m (55yd) or more in diameter, has been estimated at nearly six or seven hundred years with a growth rate of up to 35cm (14in) a year!

Fungi have always had a rather mixed reception; although for many of us they are as familiar and useful as our everyday vegetables, to a great many people they represent a very unknown world. In the past they have been condemned in parts of Europe as vile, unholy plants begotten of the devil, while in other cultures the edible species are the most treasured of all plants, the 'food of the gods'. Certainly the Romans treated them with great respect and hired trained mushroom collectors to go out and collect the safe and edible species for preparation in exotic dishes. The most highly prized were toadstools called boleti, not the same species as the boleti we know today but in fact some of the gilled species. A particular favourite was *Amanita caesarea* (see page 85). This beautiful fungus is still highly rated in the kitchen today but the Romans went to the extent of having special dishes called *boletaria* to prepare them in and only cutlery made of such materials as amber was believed suitable for eating such a delicacy. Considering that the Emperor Claudius Caesar is reputed to have died from a dish of poisoned mushrooms, it is perhaps understandable that the Romans took such pains over their preparation.

Various primitive cultures have worshipped species of fungi. The early Siberian peoples for centuries gathered the Fly Agaric Toadstool as a sacred plant. The Fly Agaric is one of a number of toadstools which contain hallucinogens and the strange visions and dreams they caused were credited as a gift from the gods. In Mexico a similar cult surviving today uses a fungus called 'Teonanactl', which is variously interpreted as 'food of the gods' or 'dangerous mushroom'.

A fungus which was definitely regarded with suspicion was the Stinkhorn, *Phallus impudicus*, and its relatives (see page 60). This suggestively shaped and repulsively odorous fungus was a natural candidate when it came to connecting fungi with witchcraft. The peculiar 'eggs' from which the mature fruit-body grows were regarded with particular suspicion as the eggs of demons and evil spirits. Even so, the eggs are eaten by some people and even today they are used as a cure for various ailments or as love potions.

As we saw at the beginning of this book, the speed with which a toadstool grows above ground is essentially an expansion of the tissues rather than true growth. Nevertheless, it is still commonly believed that *all* mushrooms and toadstools grow overnight and are gone by midday. There are many stories connecting this rapid growth rate with the full moon and also with thunder. The thunder theory is widespread in Japan where certain fungi are actually called 'thunder mushrooms'. This idea is, of course, not completely ill-founded for thunder is usually accompanied by rainstorms and fungi often do spring up after rain. There has even been serious research into whether the moon does indeed affect mushroom growth and some results, although uncertain at present, suggest that it might. The moon does after all exert a gravitational pull and fungi are known to be influenced by gravity, so perhaps the connection lies there.

Wherever one travels in the world there are fungi and stories connected with them, whether it is the natives of New Guinea who credit special properties to the strange stinkhorn, *Phallus indusiata*, with its long lace-like collarette, or people in various parts of Europe who even to this day believe that King Alfred's Cakes, *Daldinia concentrica*, are a cure for cramp. In Africa one Swahili-speaking tribe has a sort of ritual 'quiz' in which one of the standard questions is 'Who is the little man of the forest with the big hat?' The answer is, of course, a toadstool.

In myths fungi are often closely connected with the gods. They appear as a 'gift' in the tale of the Koryak peoples, who say that the god Existence spat upon the ground and the Fly Agaric appeared to give strength to the warrior Big Raven in time of need. As with many folk stories, there is a rather similar tale current in parts of Europe which says that St Peter spat bread on the ground while he was following Christ and this too turned into mushrooms. The Devil, who was close behind, also spat on the ground and made the brightly coloured but poisonous toadstools!

Previous page
Fairy rings
Rings of different-coloured grass were
in the past explained away by stories of
fire-breathing dragons scorching the
earth, or the dancing of fairies and
elves. Such rings could either bring
good or bad luck and cure or cause ills,
as well as providing love potions. To
enter one at night, under a full moon,
was to risk serious enchantment by the
elves, and woe betide the cow that ate
within the magic circle! The toadstools
at the outer edges were, strangely
enough, rarely noticed, and only in the
nineteenth century was the true
relationship between the grass ring and
the fungus discovered (see page 70).

Top left
**Marasmius oreades (Fairy Ring
Fungus)**
Although nearly all fungi can, and often
do, grow in circles, this species is the
most frequent cause of fairy rings. A
fairly small toadstool, 5–10cm (2–4in),
it has a light brown cap with a central
knob and often a slightly ridged or
milled edge; the flesh is firm and
elastic. This species is capable of drying
out in hot weather, reabsorbing
moisture when it rains and then starting
to produce spores all over again. It is a
delicious edible species which dries well
and can be cooked in a variety of ways.
It frequently forms very large rings,
many metres across, and consequently
presents problems to green-keepers on
golf courses and cricket pitches.

Bottom left
Amanita muscaria (Fly Agaric)
The most well-known toadstool in the
world, the Fly Agaric has featured in
countless children's books with the
appropriate gnome or fairy sitting on
top. It has also been the subject of both
mystical and religious worship in parts
of Russia and northern Asia. The
strange hallucinogenic drugs obtained
from the cap have for centuries been
used to induce visions, while the
poisons also contained in the fruit-body
were once used to stupefy and kill flies.
An absolutely unmistakable fungus, it
remains one of the most magnificent
species in the world. Curiously, in
North America the Fly Agaric varies in
colour from bright canary yellow to
pink or white, and only on the west
coast can the typical red form be
observed.

**Auricularia auricula
(Judas Ear, Jew's Ear)**
A remarkable fungus which looks
uncannily like a strange, velvety brown
ear, this is almost always found on elder
trees. The common name is associated
with the legend that Judas Iscariot
hanged himself on an elder tree—the
fungus is supposed to represent his
uneasy spirit returned to earth. It is one
of the jelly fungi (the tremellales) and
becomes bone hard when dry. It is
considered a delicacy and in the Far
East a closely related species is widely
cultivated as a vegetable.

Right
Dictyophora indusiata
The Phallales, or stinkhorns, have always been associated with folklore, superstitions and suspected witchcraft. Their foul odour, rapid growth and emergence from an 'egg' have all lent substance to their unfortunate reputation. In centuries past, people were actually accused of summoning demons and witches to drop these eggs into a neighbour's garden in order to cause him illness from the noxious fumes! This tropical stinkhorn species, with its fantastic lacy veil, is still today held in awe by certain tribes who believe it to have magical properties.

Left
Daldinia concentrica (King Alfred's Cakes, Cramp Balls)
This very hard, black fungus is found particularly on beeches and when cut open reveals many layers of concentric rings in the flesh. The rather sombre, burnt appearance, and the black powdery spores, closely resembling charcoal, led to the association with the legend of King Alfred's unfortunate cakes. Although the reputation of this fungus for curing cramp is widespread in Europe, it is difficult to see just how it originated, as there is no proof of its efficacy.

Right
Tremella mesenterica (Witches' Butter)
From the common name one might expect a rather nasty, unpleasant, slimy fungus, but in fact this is a very lovely and delicate species which belongs to the group called the Tremellales, or jelly fungi. The large, irregular fruit-bodies, rather like wrinkled lobes, have a soft jelly-like texture and are the most intense yellow-orange. When dry, the fungus hardens, turns dark orange and looks completely different. It is found on deciduous wood from late autumn through to early winter. A close relative, also called Witches' Butter, but more deserving of the title, is *Exidia glandulosa*. It has soft brown or black fruit-bodies and is also found on wood.

FUNGI FORAYS

In all pursuits there are correct methods of procedure, and if you follow a few simple rules then your enjoyment from collecting and examining fungi will be greatly increased. Perhaps the first question we should ask ourselves is whether we should pick them at all. In these conservation-minded times, when man is at last realizing that his environment is a unique and all too easily damaged heritage, we should think very carefully before interfering with the countryside. But there are fundamental differences between the characteristics of fungal growth and those of a wild flower, for example, and this allows us a freer approach to uprooting fungi than almost any other organism. If you pick a wild flower from the forest floor, leaves, stem and all, you have not only killed that particular plant, you have also prevented it dispersing its seeds. If you do the same to a toadstool, although you have removed that particular fruiting mechanism the underground mycelium still remains and it is this which is the actual 'body' of the fungus. The mycelium is still able to continue its growth and produce more fruit-bodies to replace the one you have picked.

The advantages of this to the person interested in toadstools is obvious: he is not killing the fungus by picking its fruiting-bodies and the habitat is not substantially altered in any way. This does not mean to say that you should rush out into the woods and pick every toadstool in sight. You should never collect more than you can study or eat at any one time, and you should remember that other people as well as you may wish to see and enjoy these plants growing in their natural habitat. You should also bear in mind that a great many creatures depend on fungi for their existence. Insects feed in and upon the fruiting-bodies of the fungi and small mammals often nibble the tender flesh, and both will be affected in some way by the destruction of their food-source. So the first consideration in collecting should always be moderation.

Whether you collect fungi to eat or to study, you should take great care how you pick them. It is all too common to see people return from an afternoon's walk with a soggy, crushed mess instead of the beautiful organisms they picked in the woods. Like wild flowers fungi are extremely fragile and will not stand up to rough handling in any degree, but unless all the many and often very delicate features of the fungi are intact when you get them home you will find great difficulty in arriving at a correct identification.

The first thing to avoid at all costs is the ubiquitous plastic bag. These otherwise useful articles are worse than useless for the majority of fungi, making the soft, rather watery fruit-bodies sweat and collapse. Another unfortunately common habit is to transport the plastic bag of fungi home in the back window of a car, where the increase in temperature helps to contribute to a wasted collecting trip. This method of collecting can also be dangerous, for such conditions are ideal for bacterial putrefaction and if the fungi are intended for eating it might cause food poisoning.

To collect properly you should first carefully prise the entire toadstool out of the soil, paying particular attention to the base of the stem which is a vital factor in identifying such fungi as the Death Cap and which if left behind could result in tragic, even fatal, misidentification. When you have the fungus intact and relatively free of soil, it should be placed in a broad, flat-bottomed basket or collecting box. If possible there should only be a single layer of fungi, but if you must collect more do take especial care to place the large, bulky species at the bottom and not on top of such delicate species as *Mycena* or *Coprinus*. Ideally these small fungi should be separated into smaller collecting boxes or into compartments within the mushroom basket. A very good method of transport is to wrap each fungus in a twist of waxed-paper, rather in the way that sweets are wrapped. This kind of paper can be purchased in rolls and you often find it used as a lining inside cardboard cereal boxes. The fungi do not sweat in this paper as they would in plastic bags, and the stiffness of the rolled paper helps to keep them from crushing each other.

Thus the three essential items for the fungus collector are an adequately sized flat basket, a knife or trowel and a supply of waxed-paper squares for important or particularly delicate specimens. If you intend to collect any of the micro-fungi a small box with compartments will also be useful. And for the larger fungi you may like to bear in mind the salutary tale of one very eminent mycologist who was once followed by two keepers from a lunatic asylum because he was carrying an axe with which to collect polypores from trees!

Once you have brought your fungus successfully home, and assuming that you do not wish only to eat them, there are a number of ways of recording and experimenting with your finds. I would urge everyone to try their hand at drawing or painting fungi. This not only provides an accurate record but also ensures that the details are impressed upon your mind, for in order to make an accurate representation of a fungus you have to examine it minutely. Many people shy away from the idea of trying to record details by pictorial means, but the drawing can be simplified so that even the most unartistic of us can make an accurate and useful record. If you cannot make an outline drawing to the correct proportions you can always cut the fungus down the middle and trace around it, and if your colouring is rather uncertain you can add notes to indicate the important features. Even the simplest of coloured drawings, combined with detailed written notes, forms a useful record for the future. The written description should always follow a regular order for ease of reference; the usual procedure is to start at the cap and work down, taking note of every distinctive feature, not forgetting smell. If you are absolutely certain that it is not one of the poisonous species, you can also record the taste by chewing a tiny piece of the fungus, but do not swallow it unless you are sure the fungus is edible.

How to recognize and split the contrasting types of fungi into easily distinguishable and natural groupings had always been a problem for the field mycologist. There are many detailed and thorough methods of identification which can be made with the help of a microscope, but when it comes to identification in the field we have to rely on larger and more easily seen features.

One microscopic feature, however, can easily be seen—the spore colour. Although a single spore is far too small to be seen with the naked eye, a thick deposit of spores forms a readily observed and valuable guide to the identification of individual species. The idea of grouping toadstools by their different spore colours was first used extensively by the famous mycologist Elias Fries in 1821, and it still forms the basis of many keys to the identification of fungi today. One might think that the colour of the gills themselves would give an indication of spore colour but in fact the two can differ greatly. It is possible to have such unlikely combinations as purple gills with white spores or blue gills with pink spores.

To examine the spore deposit, you need to take a spore 'print'. The cap of the fungus is removed from the stem and placed, gills downward, on a sheet of white paper or glass. It is then covered with an upturned beaker or similar article to prevent the tissues of the cap drying too rapidly and to exclude any air currents which could disturb the fall of the spores. After an hour or two, depending on the size of the toadstool, carefully lift the cap, taking care not to smudge the print. If the print is successful, you will see a perfect pattern of radiating lines. It is formed by the spores being projected off the gill surface and falling down between the gills on to the paper or glass, where they settle as a deposit. Fungi spores fall into one of four major colour groupings: white (varying to cream or yellow), salmon-pink, ochre or rusty-brown to cigar-brown, and purple-brown to black. There are also a few rather rare fungi with spore colours such as blue-green, red or grey-green, but the majority of your finds will come within the four main groups.

Although spore colour is widely used as a basis of classification in many field guides, it is actually a very artificial one. Grouping fungi together just because they have similar spore colour, or splitting them for the opposite reason, often gives rise to misleading ideas about the relationship between different groups of toadstools. For example, the genus *Agaricus*, which provides us with the familiar cultivated mushroom, has dark brown spores, while the closely related *Lepiota* species usually have white spores. However, as long as you bear in mind the fact that spore colour does not necessarily reflect any real relationship between different toadstools, there is no doubt that it can form a very convenient starting point to splitting them up into more manageable groups.

You can keep the spore prints of each fungus as part of your record if you spray them with a fixative such as that used on paintings. You should still make a note of the spore colour as it may fade on the print. If you intend to have the fungus examined by an expert, it would also be advisable to scrape some of the spores into a small tube or transparent envelope so that he can look at them under a microscope.

The best way to preserve the actual fruit-body of a fungus is to dry it rapidly in hot air, either in a low oven with the door open, or suspended over a radiator. The large and woody polypores will usually dry perfectly without any special treatment, other than ridding them of insects, and they make very decorative objects. Smaller toadstools can also be preserved in the drying crystals used by flower arrangers. These crystals may be obtained from a good florist and can be reused over and over again. When the dry, and by now rather shrivelled, fungus is ready it should be kept either in large envelopes or individual boxes and protected from the ravages of insects by the addition of mothballs or other slowly vapourizing insecticide.

Although fungi wll grow almost anywhere if the conditions are right, you can increase your chances of finding them by looking in certain favoured spots. Woodlands are the obvious place, but if you just plunge straight in and hope to see a large number of different species you may be disappointed. The interior of woodlands is often surprisingly poor in variety of fungi and the richest hunting grounds are the edges of the woodland or along woodland paths. If the wood adjoins a field there is the added advantage that you may also find some of the grassland species. Mixed woodlands are usually far more rewarding than pure stands of one type of tree, as many fungi grow only in association with particular trees, and often one side of a wood will be better than the other, due to such factors as exposure to sun and wind, drainage and soil.

Instead of random searching, you may wish to keep records of a specific area or habitat, such as a particular stand of trees or a forest clearing; logs and tree stumps also have their own unique fungus flora to investigate and of course each species of tree will have its own particular growth of toadstools. One of the most rewarding and useful projects is to study a small, well-defined area over several seasons. The records of fungi that you can obtain are often quite remarkable and may number many hundreds of species. Even areas which are supposedly well known may reveal dozens of new specimens simply by being examined regularly. You may like to plot the distribution of one particular species of toadstool in a small area of the forest floor and see how this changes from one year to the next.

This is particularly interesting in the case of a fairy ring; it is quite easy to work out its rate of growth by following the appearance and recovery of the bare circle of earth and the richer circle of grass. You could keep a record of the appearance of different species in relation to the weather conditions each year. Some species are said to come up in dry years and others in wet, but is this really so? Very little real information is available about many aspects of fungi and careful observations might be of real value in discovering the growth patterns of even our commoner toadstools. You might also join one of the many clubs and societies which exist for the study of fungi, or find out if your local natural history association holds fungus meetings. Many of the mycological societies arrange fungus-collecting trips every year, usually with an expert to help and instruct newcomers and this really is the best and most enjoyable way to learn your fungi.

Previous page
Dead timber is rapidly colonized by many species of fungi, such as the brackets shown here, and is a very good habitat to study. It is interesting to keep a close watch on one or two logs and observe the many different fungi that occur in succession. Do not forget to look for the very tiny slime moulds (Myxomycetes) which abound in such places. Beneath loose bark you can often see the cottony mycelium of the fungus or the strong 'bootlaces' of such species as *Armillaria mellea*.

Above
Although woodlands are the main habitat of fungi, the greatest variety of species are found on the edges of wooded areas or along paths, and comparatively few grow in deep shade. The photograph shows a typical birch and bracken woodland area, with the striking Fly Agaric (*Amanita muscaria*) so common in this kind of habitat. Note that the toadstools are still fruiting near the dead stump of a birch tree, illustrating that the mycorrhizal association between fungus and tree often continues after the tree has died.

The impressive display of fungi grouped on this table were collected in one afternoon by a group of amateur mycologists. A damp autumn day in almost any woodland of mixed trees should produce similar results, proving that there is a great variety of toadstools to be discovered if only you look for them. Among the species shown here are several boletes, amanitas, tricholomas and russulas, all of which occur quite commonly and in large numbers. For study purposes you would normally not collect so many species on one trip, as they would start to decay before you could examine them properly. It is wiser to confine yourself to picking a few species and studying them in detail.

Left
One of the most informative clues to the identification of a fungus is the attachment of the gill or pores to the stem. If you are collecting fungi to study, you should always make a vertical cross-section of the cap and stem. This will also reveal any colour changes in the flesh, and other important characteristics, such as a hollow stem. It is useful to trace round the shape if you are going to make an outline drawing to scale.

Left
Truffle Hunting
This illustration shows a truffle hunter
in the classic traditions of Europe, with
truffle pig and mushroom basket to
hand. The pig's sensitive nose can
detect truffles from a considerable
distance and soon roots them out for
his lucky owner. Indeed, the only
difficulty is in beating your pig to the
spot and preventing him from eating all
of the find! Dogs are also used and can
detect truffles at even greater distances
than a pig, but their training is more
difficult as dogs do not possess the
passion for truffles that is inherent in
the pig.

Above
**Gymnopilus junonius
(= Pholiota spectabilis)**
A large, fresh clump of this fungus is a
truly spectacular sight, with flaming,
yellow-orange caps 13–15cm (5–6in)
across set on long stout stems with
large, flaring rings. Always found on
wood in deciduous forests, it usually
attacks dying or dead trees and is only
seen at the base of the tree. This
locality has large quantities of fallen
timber and would be an ideal place to
search for all kinds of fungi.

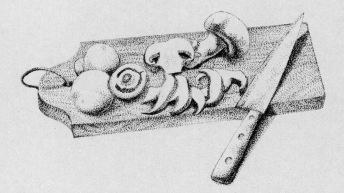

TO EAT
OR NOT TO EAT?

The use of fungi as food has had a long and chequered history, waxing and waning in popularity over the years and in different countries. Throughout most of Europe, Russia and the Far East, they form an integral part of the diet and in some of the European markets up to 300 different species are legally allowed to be offered for sale. The Russians in particular consume vast quantities of fungi, especially the *Russula* and *Lactarius* species, even those which are elsewhere considered to be far too hot and spicy. Many immigrants to North America took their eating traditions with them, including the taste for fungi. Britain alone forms a noticeable exception to the rest of Europe, with only the common field mushrooms or the cultivated species eaten at all widely.

With so many thousands of people collecting and eating wild fungi and more starting every year, it is vital that everyone is aware of the risks involved and that the correct information is readily available concerning the edible and poisonous species. Even today, when we have so much more detailed knowledge of the poisonous species, deaths are still all too regularly reported and there are no doubt many hundreds of cases of minor poisoning which go unreported each year. The reasons for this are usually the same each year: collectors rely on local traditions and rule-of-thumb procedures to distinguish poisonous from edible fungi and this simply isn't good enough. Such well-known and commonly used 'rules' as peeling the cap, poisonous species turning silver black or only eating fungi that grow in fields have absolutely no foundation in fact. The Death Cap will pass most 'tests' and still kill you! Only a thorough knowledge of the edible species you wish to collect will ensure safety and to be doubly sure you should also be aware of the important characteristics of the poisonous species.

This does not mean that you should be unnecessarily alarmist about the poisonous species; there are a great many tried and tested fungi which are eaten regularly the world over and which are quite easily recognized without risk of error.

The edible species greatly outnumber the poisonous, although there is of course a considerable variation in their taste value, ranging from such epicurean delights as the Cep (*Boletus edulis*) or the Morels (*Morchella* species) to the equally edible but rather bland species which will form the bulk of a day's collecting.

It is only when you start to branch out into the more obscure species that mistakes are liable to happen, and mistakes in fungi collecting can have fatal results. Many collectors think they are safe if they stick to the true wood and field mushrooms, the various *Agaricus* species. By doing this they run the risk of collecting some of the not so edible 'doubles' that exist. If they had kept instead to the more exotic, but therefore more easily recognized, favourites—the boletes, parasols and morels—such mistakes would almost certainly not have taken place. The common Field Mushroom can be surprisingly difficult for the beginner to identify properly and victims of the Death Cap are on record as saying that they picked it because it looked like a mushroom.

The rules mentioned in the last chapter are even more

important when you intend to eat your finds. To collect the fungus intact and so reveal any telltale signs such as a volva is vital for accurate identification. The golden rule is: if you are at all unsure of a mushroom's identity, *don't* eat it. Most fungi are best eaten young, but do not collect 'buttons' which are too small to identify accurately—they may belong to another, less edible species. Ideally you should at first stay with the five or six really well-known and delicious edible species illustrated on the following pages: the Cep, Morel, Parasol, Shaggy Inkcap, Chanterelle and Black-Trumpet (*Craterellus*). These are all very distinctive and even a beginner can soon recognize them very quickly. Once you are thoroughly acquainted with these, you may then wish to go on to try some of the many other popular edible species, such as the Beefsteak Fungus (*Fistulina hepatica*), the Oyster Fungus (*Pleurotus ostreatus*), the Blewits (*Lepista nudum*), *Lactarius deliciosus*, and the many edible species of bolete. It is a great advantage if your initial trips are with a mycological society or other experts who can identify these at first hand and show you their distinguishing features in the field.

When you have your fungus identified and ready for cooking, do make use of a good cook book. There are several specialist fungi books available, and they really are useful; a mushroom cooked incorrectly can end up quite tasteless and you may never realize its full potential. If you are still dubious about collecting your own food but would like to try the more unusual kinds, you can often find canned or dried fungi in Italian, Chinese or Japanese food shops and these are, of course, quite safe!

Fungi are usually eaten as a vegetable rather than as a main dish, for their great virtue is complementing and bringing out the flavour of other foods. They are particularly good with meat, but they are also a valuable addition to stews, soups and omelettes, and as an ingredient in stuffings, sauces and hors d'oeuvres. Nutritionally the boletes in particular provide significant amounts of protein, and many species also contain useful vitamins (B, D and A), as well as various trace elements and minerals. It is known that people and animals have survived for extensive periods on fungi alone with no ill effects, sometimes even gaining in weight!

In preparing fungi it is important to examine them carefully, remove any dirt or insects, and cut away soft or rotten portions of the fruit-body. A slice down the centre of the fungus will reveal any insects or larvae within; unfortunately insect attack is fairly likely, especially in the more mature fruit-bodies. Do not wash them more than is absolutely necessary—usually a wipe with a cloth will suffice. Only peel the cap where the skin is very thick or has a glutinous surface; scales are usually left on as they normally vanish with cooking. Whether or not you eat the stem depends on the species and how tough it is; with tender species you will only need to cut off the base and remove any soil.

Do not eat too many fungi at once, particularly if you have never eaten that species before. Many people find even the best edible species rather indigestible and some unfortunates are allergic to all fungi and can become quite ill or develop a rash. So wait until you are sure of your body's tolerances.

The fervour and enthusiasm which many people have for eating fungi can seem quite amazing to those who do not indulge, and to accompany a group of devoted mycologists one might think that precious gems were at stake! Particularly where the Morel is concerned, competition is very strong, and in Europe, where the truffle commands a high price, a man with truffles on his land is a very wealthy man indeed.

Although it is to be hoped that encounters with poisonous fungi will not be in a meal, they are nevertheless a fascinating group of plants and anyone intending to eat fungi must become acquainted with them. The various toxins contained within the fungus vary in their chemical make-up and in their effects upon man, and because of this it is

possible to group the poisonous species according to the toxins they contain.

Firstly comes the most complex and deadly of the toxins and hence the most infamous of the toadstools. These are the various *Amanita* species and in particular the Death Cap, *A.phalloides*, and the Destroying Angel, *A.virosa*. These two species, along with one or two close relatives, cause a high proportion of the really serious and often deadly poisonings each year. The toxins contained in the fruit-bodies of these fungi are unequalled for their complexity and their lethal qualities; recent research suggests the presence of up to eleven different, closely related poisonous chemicals belonging to two principal groups—the phallotoxins and the amatoxins, the two groups of poison differing in their effects and in the time they take to attack the body. One of the difficulties with treating Death Cap poisoning is that it usually takes six to fifteen hours, sometimes even longer, before the symptoms appear and by the time the symptoms are apparent it is too late to use a stomach pump as the poisons have already entered the bloodstream. The effects of the poisoning are long and painful, with severe gastric and abdominal pains accompanied by violent vomiting. If treatment is not obtained death will occur within three to five days, and post-mortem examination normally reveals severe liver and kidney damage. The exact workings of the toxins are still not fully understood, although it is known that they are not filtered out of the body by the kidneys as are other harmful substances, and that they attack and break down the walls of the body cells as well as causing the gastric upsets. Until recently, in the absence of a completely successful antidote the only treatment was to attempt to counteract the symptoms as they occurred. In some recent cases, however, the use of the drug thioctic acid and of artificial kidney machines (blood dialysis units) has had notable success and it appears that we have at last found an effective treatment for Death Cap poisoning.

Luckily such deadly poisons are rare within the fungus world and only a few other toadstools are known to contain them. Two which have caused some poisonings are *Galerina autumnalis* and the closely related species *G.marginata* (*unicolor*). These two rather small brown mushrooms are thankfully not very common and are usually passed over by collectors as being too small to eat. But they can be mistaken for edible species, in particular *Galerina* (= *Pholiota*) *mutabilis* which is commonly eaten; both species have a ring on the stem, and are rather similar in general appearance.

Although the majority of the species of *Amanita* seem to be more or less poisonous, not all of them contain the same poisons as the Death Cap, and two particularly well-known species have a different sort of poison altogether. These are the Fly Agaric, *Amanita muscaria*, and the Panther Cap, *A.pantherina*, which are but two of a whole range of fungi containing the poison muscarine. This poison is also widely distributed in the genera *Inocybe* and *Clitocybe*, some of which are even more potent than the two amanitas. The effects of muscarine poisoning are not usually fatal except when it has been taken in very large doses; the normal reaction to eating one or two of these fungi is a reduced heart rate, giddiness and blurred vision, sweating and difficulty in breathing, as well as stomach cramps and vomiting. The poisoning is further complicated in the Fly Agaric by the presence of another type of drug, this time an hallucinogen, musrazone. Hallucinogenic drugs of one sort or other are curiously quite frequent in fungi, and the genera *Psilocybe* and *Panaeolus* both contain chemicals that effect the brain in a very similar fashion to the now famous drug L.S.D. The fungus *Psilocybe semilanceata*, a very common grassland species was recently the subject of a court case where a man was charged with being in possession of a dangerous drug. He was found not guilty, the judge deciding that being in possession of a drug and being in possession of a mushroom, albeit containing a drug, were two different things! Needless to say the use of any of these fungi for their hallucinogenic properties is highly dangerous, as most of them also contain the poison muscarine, along

Previous page
Boletus edulis (Cep, Penny Bun)
The prince of edible fungi, this delicacy
has been appreciated by lovers of fine
food since the Romans hired special
collectors to find them and chefs to
prepare them. The large, fat brown
fruit-bodies, often weighing several
kilos, are gathered by the thousand in
Europe for cooking and for drying to
flavour packet soups! Most boletes are
edible and only a few are bitter or
suspected of causing upsets. The Cep
is hard to confuse with any other
species and is found in both pine and
deciduous woodlands throughout the
autumn. The tubes are usually
removed before cooking although this is
not necessary when the fungi are young;
the stem is also often removed
altogether or finely diced before
cooking.

Below
**Lepiota procera
(Parasol Mushroom)**
A tall, graceful and quite unmistakeable
fungus, the Parasol Mushroom is
eagerly sought after for food. When
fried, the caps are quite delicious and so
large that they often fill a frying pan! It
is found in fields near trees, or in
woodland clearings. The often very tall
stem has numerous horizontal, brownish
markings, rather like fine snakeskin or
zebra stripes. The cap has a prominent
knob in the centre and is covered with
fine woolly scales. The cap colour is a
pale fawn or brown, with the stem
slightly darker, and the stem has a
prominent, moveable ring. When it is
young the closed caps on the tall stems
resemble large drumsticks and they can
often be spotted from a great distance.

with other suspect chemicals.

A rather strange reaction is caused by the species
Coprinus atramentarius, but what is even stranger is that the
reaction only occurs after alcohol has been drunk with the
meal. When this reaction was first reported it was realized
that it was very similar to that of a drug used in treating
alcoholics, Antabuse, which causes an unpleasant reaction
every time the patient has a drink. The exact identity of the
chemical in the fungus had long eluded scientists and the
exact conditions necessary for poisoning to take place were
uncertain, but Swedish researchers have recently isolated
the chemical, which they call coprine, and it seems likely
that the reaction only takes place if the fungus is cooked.
The symptoms, although not serious, are distressing and
involve an intense flushing of the face and neck, together
with an increased pulse rate and a feeling of great heat.
These symptoms usually fade quite rapidly, although they
may return if more alcohol is drunk.

One of the most remarkable toxins is surely that contained
within the False Morel, *Gyromitra esculenta*. From its species
name you might infer that this is a very choice edible species
and indeed it is widely eaten in Europe. However, cases have
occurred, some of them fatal, of poisoning caused by this
very same fungus. The answer to this strangely variable
reaction, which has puzzled mycologists for some time, lies
in the fact that it contains rocket fuel! Impossible as it may
seem, *Gyromitra esculenta* naturally produces a chemical
called monomethylhydrazine which is manufactured by man
as a rocket fuel. This chemical compound has a boiling point
of about 87°C, so that if the fungus is first boiled in water at
100°C the poison will be evaporated out of the tissues.
However if the temperature is not high enough or the fungus
is not cooked long enough then enough poison can remain to
cause serious harm.

Finally, there are a number of species which can cause
severe gastric upsets, although not usually anything more
serious. These include many of the *Russula* and *Lactarius*
species (although these are usually rendered harmless after
cooking), and various species of *Tricholoma*, *Boletus* and
even *Agaricus*. The latter may seem surprising when you
consider that *Agaricus hortensis*, the cultivated mushroom,
provides us with our principle fungus food. One *Agaricus*
species in particular seems to cause trouble—*Agaricus
anthodermus*, the Yellow-stainer. As its name implies, this
fungus stains vivid yellow, particularly when the flesh is
broken at the base of the stem, and although many people
can eat this species quite safely others are made very ill
indeed. The yellow stains and rather flattened, slightly scaly
cap are usually quite easily detected and separate this
species from the common Field Mushroom, *Agaricus
campestris*.

As well as the danger from these different types of
poisoning, you must also remember that like other vegetables
the fungi are susceptible to decay and to avoid the risk of
food poisoning they should only be used when they are fresh.
Avoid any fungi that have been caught by frost, for species
which are otherwise quite edible can suddenly prove
dangerous.

If all these warnings of poisoning sound alarming,
remember that the truly poisonous species are very much in
the minority and that with common sense and strict
identification you can enjoy some of Nature's most subtle
flavours, not only good food but free food!

Right
Amanita virosa (Destroying Angel)
A beautiful but deadly fungus, this
species is as poisonous as the closely
related Death Cap. The entire fruit-
body is pure white and taller, as well as
more graceful, than that of the Death
Cap. It can reach 30cm (1ft) in height
and is quite lovely when seen in the
pine or birch woods that it favours. In
Europe it is found mainly in the colder
regions and thus is commoner in the
north. It is particularly common in
North America, where the Death Cap
is rather scarce.

Far right, top
**Amanita caesarea (Caesar's
Mushroom)**
A large and beautifully coloured
species, Caesar's Mushroom has long
been in favour as a delicacy and was
reputed to have been the particular
favourite of the Roman Emperors—
thus the specific name of *caesarea*. The
clear orange cap, with large fragments
of veil tissue left on top, and the yellow
gills and stem are unmistakeable. The
white volva is particularly well
developed. It has a definite preference
for warmer climates and although quite
common in Europe has not yet been
reported in England. In North America
there is a rather more slender, closely
related species, with a distinct knob in
the centre of the cap.

Far right, bottom
Amanita phalloides (Death Cap)
The Death Cap is certainly the most
notorious and one of the most poisonous
of all fungi. Containing numerous
toxins which attack various organs of
the body, it has caused more deaths
than almost any other species of fungi.
The cap is usually olive green or
yellow-green, but it can also be almost
white or brown and it is then that it
may be confused with an edible
mushroom by the unwary. However, if
the telltale features of completely
uniform white gills, ring on the stem
and volva at the base are present, then
no-one need fear making a mistake. It
prefers the shade of oak woods and is
rarely seen in more open places. In
favourable years it may appear in large
numbers.

Overleaf
Coprinus comatus (Shaggy Mane, Lawyer's Wig)
A very common and delicious edible fungus, this is possibly the safest of all fungi for the inexperienced to collect. Its tall, conical fruit-body is unmistakable, with a white, woolly surface and thin stem with a narrow ring. It is often found in large numbers on roadsides, rubbish tips or wherever the ground contains a quantity of organic material. Picked before the caps start to dissolve into fluid, these mushrooms have a very delicate flavour and texture.

Calocybe (= Tricholoma) gambosum (St George's Mushroom)
Found in spring about the time of St George's Day (April 23), it is difficult to confuse this fungus with any other spring species. The large, meaty fruit bodies are white or ivory in colour, looking rather like Field Mushrooms, except that the gills and spores are also white, whereas those of the Field Mushroom are brown. The flesh has a very distinctive smell of new meal or even slightly of cucumber, and is very tasty when cooked. This mushroom is quite common in grassy clearings and fields, often occurring in large numbers. Its name has been changed because it is no longer considered a true *Tricholoma* as there are differences in structure and the flesh reacts differently to certain chemicals.

Right
Amanita pantherina (Panther Cap)
This is a rather uncommon species which is easily confused with the much more common *Amanita excelsa*, or even the Blusher, *A.rubescens*. The cap is greyish-brown with prominent white 'warts', the remains of the universal veil. The stem has a ring and at the base is the most important distinguishing feature—one, two, or even three, rings of tissue clinging to the stem. These are the remains of the veil which are left behind after the stem has expanded. It is a dangerously poisonous species, containing large amounts of the toxin muscarine which can kill in large doses. Panther Caps are found in all sorts of woodlands.

Left
Agaricus campestris (Field Mushroom)
This fungus is known by almost everyone who has ever picked mushrooms in the fields. The rather small white or brownish caps are seen only in open grassland and pasture, never in woodlands. The gills when young are a bright pink but rapidly turn grey, then brown, as the spores mature. This is an important feature to look for when in doubt of authenticity, as is the delicate ring on the stem. The stem itself is rather short, often less than the width of the cap, 5–10cm (2–4in), and never has a volva at the base like the poisonous *Amanita* species. Cooked for generations by country folk all over Europe, it really needs no introduction and most cookery books have at least one recipe for it.

Right
Cantharellus cibarius (Chanterelle)
This most attractive fungus almost
cries out to be eaten, and for once its
promise of edibility is not deceptive.
The fleshy fruit-bodies have delicate
orange tints and smell deliciously of
apricots when they are fresh. After
Boletus edulis, the Chanterelle is
perhaps the most sought-after edible
species and appears in markets all over
Europe. If you look at the undersurface
of the top-shaped cap you will see that
it lacks true gills, merely having folded
wrinkles, and in fact it is closer in
structure to the club fungi. This species
favours damp, mossy woodlands, either
pine or deciduous, and usually occurs in
large groups.

Far right, top
Cortinarius orellanus
Although often overlooked, this rather
nondescript fungus has been shown to
be a dangerously poisonous species,
possibly equal to the infamous Death
Cap. It may even be considered more
dangerous because the symptoms only
occur several days after the fungus is
eaten. It is not an easy species to
recognize and shows once again that
you should not eat any small toadstools
which you cannot identify correctly.

Far right, bottom
**Hygrophoropsis aurantiaca
(False Chanterelle)**
The False Chanterelle is exceedingly
common on heathland soils under birch
and bracken, and indeed it is far more
common than the true Chanterelle. The
cap may be white or orange and the
gills are sharp-edged, unlike the blunt
wrinkles of the real Chanterelle.
Although once considered poisonous,
the False Chanterelle is in fact merely
rather tasteless but is best avoided.
When there are so many other delicious
edible species it seems foolish to risk
eating more dubious fungi. The real
Chanterelle much prefers damp mossy
ground in beech or pine woods and
is rarely seen in company with the
False Chanterelle.

Morchella esculenta (Morel)
The morels form a remarkable group
which prefer the spring for the
production of their fruit-bodies. These
look rather like a bath-sponge set upon
a stalk and are generally pale brown to
grey in colour. A particularly delicious,
edible fungus, it can be prepared in a
number of different ways, and because
the fruit-bodies are hollow, they are
ideal for stuffing. Morels tend to grow
in large groups but are unfortunately
rather difficult to find. They are
members of the Ascomycetes group,
which means that the spores are
contained within special cells called
asci, from which they are ejected when
mature. These cells cover the entire
outer surface of the spongy cap.

Russula emetica
This intense scarlet toadstool belongs to
a very large group of fungi, in which
just about every colour and shade of the
spectrum is produced and a few more
besides! The *Russula* species are a
bewildering group with many species
looking exactly the same at first glance,
and differing only in minute detail.
R.emetica is one of the few fungi that
is relatively easy to identify as it grows
only under pines, and the cap is a pure
red (never pinkish or purple as are
many other species) while the stem and
gills are completely white—a dazzling
contrast! It has an extremely hot,
burning taste and it is quite inedible
when raw, although said by some to be
edible after cooking. The related species
R.mairei occurs under beeches and is
almost identical except for a greenish
reflection to the gills and a fragrant
odour.

Right
Langermannia (= Calvatia = Lycoperdon) gigantea (Giant Puffball)
Truly a giant among puffballs, this species usually reaches the size of a football but unusual specimens can attain much larger proportions. The flesh is delicious and much sought after when the fruit-body is young, before the spore mass has begun to mature and turn powdery. It grows in fields and hedgerows and seems to show a particular liking for banks and ditches, so roadsides often provide very profitable hunting grounds. The spores disperse when the tough skin gradually breaks down and peels away.

Left
Agaricus arvensis (Horse Mushroom)
This well-known and attractive edible species is commonly found in fields and woodland clearings and looks like a very large, tall Field Mushroom. Identification points to look for are gills turning dark brown, a pendant double ring or collar on the stem and the absence of a warning volva at the base of the stem. Peeling the cap is *not* a test of a true mushroom—the Death Cap also peels! Care should be taken to avoid picking the very similar Yellow-staining Mushroom, *A.xanthodermus*, which might cause an upset stomach. *A.xanthodermus* may be recognized by the immediate and intense chrome-yellow stains which appear at the base of the stem when it is cut.

Lactarius deliciosus

The name is something of a misnomer because, although widely gathered for food, this species is not particularly delicious and does not compare well with most of the other edible fungi. However, the cap is so distinctive that it can be safely recommended to the inexperienced collector. Beginning as a clear orange when fresh, the whole fungus soon develops green stains in the flesh and green bands around the margin of the cap. The gills are a deeper orange and when broken display a character typical of all the members of the genus *Lactarius*, exuding a milky fluid. In the case of this species the 'milk' is bright orange and soon turns deep green! Altogether an unmistakable fungus and a good species for beginners to experiment with.

Right

Craterellus cornucopiodes
(Horn of Plenty)

Though a very sombre and almost ugly species, the Horn of Plenty is nevertheless highly rated for its spicy flavour, particularly as it dries so well and can be ground up and used like pepper. It has the additional advantage of being quite unmistakable with its deep, trumpet-shaped fruit-bodies. It is frequently found in large groups on the leaf litter under beech trees in the autumn, but can be very hard to spot as it camouflages well!

Mushroom market
Enormous quantities of boletes,
particularly *Boletus edulis*, are collected
annually in Europe either for
immediate sale or to be dried and
added to soups. Vegetable markets such
as this market in France present an
amazing and mouthwatering sight, with
crates and crates of fruit-bodies, either
sliced or whole. On the bottom right
you can see a crate of *Lactarius
deliciosus* with their typical orange caps
and greenish stains. The enormous size
of some of the boletes also makes them
stand out from the rest!

Left
**Lepista (= Tricholoma) nudum
(Wood Blewit)**
As the growing season comes to an end
and the first frosts arrive, then is the
time to search for Blewits. On roadsides,
under piles of leaves, and on compost
or rubbish tips, in fact wherever the
soil is rich in rotted organic matter,
they are likely to fruit, usually in large
numbers. The caps are brownish but
the gills and stem are a lovely clear lilac
or lavender, while the spores are very
pale pink. They are one of the most
delicious and easily identifiable species
of fungi and well worth trying fried,
stewed, baked or in a soup. As the flesh
is often very moist they should be
cooked in only a little fat. Their
delicate flavour and meaty texture will
soon make them a firm favourite.

95

INDEX

Figures in italics refer to illustrations

ACKNOWLEDGEMENTS

The publishers wish to thank the following individuals and organizations for their kind permission to reproduce the photographs in this book:

A-Z Botanical Collection Ltd. (W. W. Roberts) 12–13 above, 40–41; R. Andrews 48 below; Heather Angel 11, 13, 14–15, 16, 18, 31, 48 above, 54 above, 67 below, 79, 86–87, 95 below; Aquila Photography 19, 60 above; Ardea Photographics 28; Biofotos (Gordon Dickson) 65; S. C. Bisserot 44, 48–49, 68–69, 77; John Burton 18–19, 74–75, 78 above; Bruce Coleman (S. C. Porter) 28–29; Eric Crichton 4, 91 below; Brian Hawkes front and back jacket, 12–13 below, 18, 20 above, 20 below, 21 below, 22 above, 23 below, 24 below, 27 above, 27 below, 42–43, 44–45, 53 above, 58, 67 above, 80–81, 84, 92–93; Philippe Joly 2–3, 22–23, 34–35, 36–37, 37, 55, 62–63, 64 below, 73 below, 89, 90–91, 95 below; Frank W. Lane/H. Schrempp 85 above; Claude Nardin 40, 46–47, 64 above, 66, 91 above; NHPA (H. R. Allen) 26 below, 30 below, 72 below, 92, (James Carmichael) 56–57, (Christine Foord) 94 above, (Brian Hawkes) 17, 24 above, 32, 83, 85 below, 93 above, 94 below, (G. E. Hyde) 30 above, 39 below, 54 below, 59, 60 below, 62, 88 above, 88 below, (Roy D. Mackay) 73 above, (K. G. Preston-Mafham) endpapers, 50–51, (H. C. F. Proctor) 33 above, 33 below, (Dr. D. A. Reid) 53 below, (G. Wall) 93 below; Natural Science Photos (P. A. Bowman) 21 above, (J. A. Grant) 1, (Alfred Leutscher) 72 above, (P. H. Ward) 6–7; Paul Richens 23 above, 26 above, 38–39, 78 below left; P. Stiles 9, 39 above, 45, 71 above; Top Agence (J. N. Reichel) 78 below right; Topham (Windridge) 25, ZEFA 70–71.